What goes the City?

CW00494735

Fourth edition

NICHOLAS RITCHIE, M.A.(Oxon)
Eton College, Windsor

Woodhead-Faulkner · Cambridge
in association with Lloyds Bank

Woodhead-Faulkner Ltd
Fitzwilliam House, 32 Trumpington Street
Cambridge CB2 1QY, England
and 51 Washington Street, Dover, NH 03820, USA

First published 1975
Second edition 1978
Third edition 1981
Fourth edition 1986

British Library Cataloguing in Publication Data
Ritchie, Nicholas
    What goes on in the City?—4th ed.
    1. Financial institutions—England—London
    I. Title   II. Lloyds Bank
    332.1'09421'2   HG186.G7

ISBN 0-85941-321-7
ISBN 0-85941-322-5 (Pbk)

Library of Congress Cataloging in Publication Data
Ritchie, Nicholas
    What goes on in the City?

    Bibliography: p.
    1. Financial institutions—England—London
2. Finance—England—London.   3. Finance—Great
Britain.   I. Title.
HG186.G7R53   1986   332.1'09421'2   85-24641

ISBN 0-85941-321-7
ISBN 0-85941-322-5 (Pbk)

Phototypeset by Wyvern Typesetting Ltd, Bristol
Printed by The Thetford Press Ltd, Thetford and London

Foreword

by Sir Jeremy Morse, K.C.M.G.
Chairman, Lloyds Bank Plc

I am pleased to write a foreword to the latest edition of this very useful book explaining the City, and I do so from an office in the heart of it.

The City, on the map, is an area of a square mile or so in the oldest part of London, first built up by the Romans, and presided over since 1191 by the Lord Mayor. It is a natural trading centre founded on the Port of London.

Over the centuries many markets have clustered here, dealing in commodities and money, and many banks and insurance companies have established their main offices here. So 'the City', as a technical term, has come to stand for the financial system of this country and the people who work in it. But it is important to remember that the financial system is in fact spread through offices and branches over the whole country.

Every major country has a financial centre. The City is the largest and most comprehensive – and, with New York, the most important – financial centre in the modern world. It not only serves the British public, industry and Government: by selling its services also to foreigners it makes a big contribution to our 'invisible' exports.

Naturally enough there are some special factors that have helped the City to achieve its pre-eminence. I would pick out the following: its key geographical position on the edge of Europe nearest to America; its use of the world's foremost language; its continuing inventiveness in constructing and improving markets; and its willingness to deal on trust with a minimum of paperwork, exemplified in the famous motto of The Stock Exchange: 'My word is my bond.'

All this is explained and illustrated in much more detail in the following nine chapters. When you have read them, I hope that you will have a better understanding of what goes on in the City and why those who work there are proud to do so.

Acknowledgements

I am indebted to many people for their kind assistance in the preparation of this little book: in particular, to my father for reading the manuscript and making helpful comments on it, and to Miss Audrey White for typing (and re-typing) it.

In order to obtain first-hand information I visited many City institutions and I would like to acknowledge especially the help given to me by Mr P.D. Bowman, Lloyds Bank Plc (Head Office); Mr J.C. Luxmoore, MBE, Baltic Exchange; Mr T. Atkins, Lloyd's of London; Mr R.J. Vardy and Mr A. Rossenburg, Union Discount Company of London Ltd; Mrs T. Murray, Banking Information Service; Mr R. K. Millett, The London Metal Exchange; Ms J. Hill, The London Commodity Exchange; Miss T.A. Burke, The Bank of England; Miss J. Kent, Chartered Insurance Institute; Mr C. Symonds, The Stock Exchange; Mr E.J. Dewbery, British Insurance Association; Mr J.M. Evans, Accepting Houses Committee; Mr J.R.C. Guy, N.M. Rothschild & Sons Ltd.

Grateful acknowledgement for permission to reproduce photographs is due to the following: Aerofilms Ltd, page 15 and cover; The Baltic Exchange, page 83; The Bank of England, pages 19, 20, 24 and 26; the Bank of Tokyo, page 78; Hill Samuel Group, pages 53, 56 and cover; Lloyd's of London, pages 60, 63, 65 and 66; The London Metal Exchange, page 84; The Stock

Exchange, pages 71, 74 and cover; Union Discount Company of London Ltd., pages 30 and 33.

N.B.R.

Contents

1 The City

The City of London is proud of its history and traditions. All over the 'square mile' – a popular phrase used to refer to the City – are scenes to delight the casual sightseer. In the busy thoroughfares dark suits still predominate, bowler hats are now less common, but there is still the occasional top hat. In the shadows of lofty, stone-faced portals stand liveried doorkeepers, ready at an instant to swing open heavy brass doors or to direct the perplexed to the correct address.

All these very commonplace sights in the City are reminders of a glorious and prosperous history, stretching back well before the Romans came and built their wall round the little settlement which already existed on the north bank of the Thames. This wall ran from Ludgate Hill in the west, northwards across Newgate Street and eastwards along the road we now call London Wall. After that it turns south in a wide arc which takes it through Jewry and on, almost due south now, into the Tower of London itself.

As an important seaport facing the Continent, but with easy access to the high seas as well, London's destiny as a trading centre was assured from early times. In the seventeenth century, English commerce took great strides forward: our modern Stock Exchange traces its origins to the 1670s, Lloyd's Insurance Corporation to the coffee house of Edward Lloyd in the 1680s, and the Bank of England was founded in 1694. The Italian ports of Genoa and

Venice, famous for their medieval commercial and financial power, were still very important at this time, but Antwerp and Bruges were establishing themselves as competitors in European commerce.

The eighteenth century saw a protracted struggle between London and the Lowland ports, in particular, for supremacy until the Napoleonic wars settled the matter in favour of the English. Industrialisation in Britain was also just getting under way on a large scale and this, besides further encouraging London's role in shipping and merchanting, helped to expand her business as a capital market and as a source of finance for foreign trade.

The power and prosperity of the British Empire, and with it the City of London, increased steadily throughout the eighteenth and nineteenth centuries. The sheer financial dominance of the City at the end of this period is illustrated by the fact that in 1913 Britain's private overseas investments had topped £3,700 million. Allowing for inflation between then and now, that total was worth then much more than today's total of foreign investments is worth now. Hand in hand with Britain's superiority in trade and shipping at this time went a currency that was accepted in settlement of all types of debt all over the world.

The present century has been a time of continual and sometimes painful adjustments for the City, as for the country at large. It was clearly impossible that so tiny an island could go on controlling such a large share of the world's trade. As other countries became industrialised they were bound to take a part in commerce that reflected their size and their natural wealth. America has emerged as a 'super-power', a class in which Britain, individually, just cannot afford to compete; not surprisingly, New York has grown as a financial centre to rival London, but it has not overtaken it.

Perhaps more than any other part of the United Kingdom, the City has responded vigorously to the challenge of the new conditions, especially since the Second World War. The City's annual net earnings from abroad are now in excess of £4,500 million, over five times what they were a decade ago. These 'invisible' earnings are vitally necessary, because very often Britain spends more money on foreign foods than foreigners spend on British exports. About a quarter of this total was provided by insurance premiums. London is also the centre of the Euro-currency markets which have sprung up in the last two decades. In banking, the network of branches and representatives of British-owned banks is many times the size of that of the American world network and earns more than £1,500 million from abroad. In the commodity markets and the Baltic Exchange, the City has the bulk of the world's dealings in basic commodities and in shipping tonnage for charter passing through its hands.

Because Britain is very dependent on her foreign trade and has many historic commitments abroad, it is natural that much attention in the City is focused on the international scene. But, of course, the City is also the centre of finance for internal commerce of all sorts. Its chief task here, as with international trade, is to bring together lenders and borrowers, so that those who need money to carry on their business can find it and those who have money but do not need it at once do not have to hold it idle. Without this matching up of borrowers and lenders, a great deal of business could not take place.

The actual 'heart of the City' is only a little over a quarter of a mile across and yet this contains the Bank of England and the Mansion House of the Lord Mayor, most of the major banks, The Stock Exchange with brokers' offices, the discount houses and quite a few insurance companies as well as Lloyd's of London, the commodity markets and the Baltic Exchange.

This crowding together in a very small area, for all its problems of accommodation, has the very great advantage that those who need to be can be in personal touch with one another very quickly and easily. It is a point that is often made particularly about the various exchanges in the City, e.g. the stock market, the commodity markets, the Baltic and Lloyd's, and we will return to it again. But what is true of those institutions is also true of the City as a whole which is, really, one vast market-place for numerous 'commodities'. Where else in the world are there markets for so many services collected together in such a small area? Of course, the

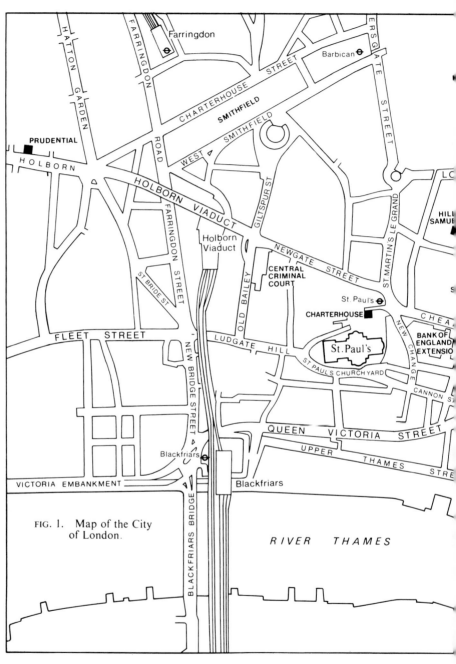

FIG. 1.   Map of the City of London.

Map of the City of London

12

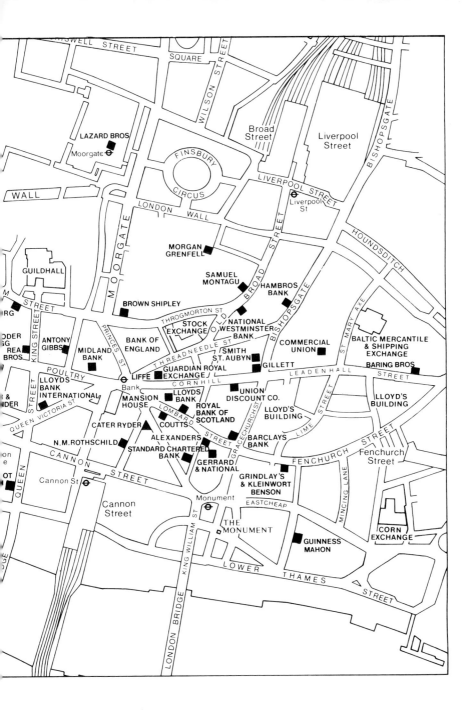

CROSSWELL STREET
SQUARE
WILSON STREET
LAZARD BROS
Moorgate
WALL
FINSBURY CIRCUS
LONDON WALL
Broad Street
Liverpool Street
LIVERPOOL STREET
Liverpool St
BISHOPSGATE
HOUNDSDITCH
MORGAN GRENFELL
GUILDHALL
M STREET
RG
SAMUEL MONTAGU
BROWN SHIPLEY
THROGMORTON ST
HAMBROS BANK
BROAD STREET
BISHOPSGATE
ST MARY AXE
ODER
GG
REA
BROS
ANTONY GIBBS
MIDLAND BANK
PRINCES ST
BANK OF ENGLAND
THREADNEEDLE ST
STOCK EXCHANGE
OLD
NATIONAL WESTMINSTER BANK
SMITH ST. AUBYN
GUARDIAN ROYAL EXCHANGE
GILLETT
COMMERCIAL UNION
LEADENHALL
BALTIC MERCANTILE & SHIPPING EXCHANGE
BARING BROS
STREET
POULTRY
KING STREET
LIFFE
Bank
CORNHILL
LLOYD'S BUILDING
LLOYDS BANK INTERNATIONAL
&
DER
MANSION HOUSE
LLOYDS BANK
UNION DISCOUNT CO.
QUEEN VICTORIA ST
LOMBARD
ROYAL BANK OF SCOTLAND
LLOYD'S BUILDING
LIME STREET
CATER RYDER
COUTTS
GRACECHURCH ST
STREET
N.M.ROTHSCHILD
ALEXANDERS
STANDARD CHARTERED BANK
BARCLAYS BANK
CANNON
on
e
CANNON STREET
GERRARD & NATIONAL
FENCHURCH
Fenchurch Street
OT
Cannon St
Cannon Street
MINCING LANE
GRINDLAY'S & KLEINWORT BENSON
Monument
KING WILLIAM ST
EASTCHEAP
THE MONUMENT
GUINNESS MAHON
CORN EXCHANGE
LOWER THAMES STREET
LONDON BRIDGE

13

telephone has made a big impact, but it is no substitute for personal contact. Perhaps its greatest contributions have been to reduce the tedious leg work of messengers, and to increase informal contacts between individuals at all levels, vital for the acquisition and dissemination of information. So much in the City depends on speed and secrecy: but these in turn require unquestioning acceptance of verbal promises, and it is doubtful if such a system could be maintained without the personal relationships which are built up over meals and at odd times throughout the day.

Altogether, some 360,000 people earn their living in the City but only about 8,000 actually live there. Three hundred years ago it had a population of 250,000 people, as is evidenced by the many ancient churches that can be seen nestling cheek by jowl with the office blocks. Now, however, with land rents so high, space for beds and kitchens and other necessities of a comfortable home is hard to afford. Companies have even begun to take 'long, hard looks' at their corridor space and to wonder how some of it, designed in a more 'spacious' age, can be better employed. Others, fortunate enough not to be tied to historic buildings of grand proportions, have been building upwards to make the most use of the small land area available.

The Government and the City

The Government has two main connections with the City, as a major borrower and as overseer through its agent, the Bank of England. The Bank was founded to manage the Government's debt and that is still a principal function but, in the nineteenth century, it assumed the additional role of being the leading City institution, largely by taking the initiative and coming to the aid of other institutions which were in financial difficulties. Now the Governor of the Bank is responsible to the Government, in a general way, for how the City conducts its affairs and he keeps closely in touch with the Treasury in Whitehall. It has been suggested that Government control of the City should be somewhat increased by the nationalisation of banks and other large financial institutions, and

An aerial view of the City of London

that this step would improve the flow of funds to manufacturing industry for much-needed investment, but at the moment only the Bank of England itself is State-owned. The City in general prizes its independence very highly, and is usually careful to follow the wishes of the Bank.

In order to investigate the functioning of the country's financial institutions the Government set up a committee under the chairmanship of Sir Harold Wilson. The progress report of this committee, issued in December 1977, found that there were no grounds for the allegation that the City has failed industry by withholding funds from worthwhile projects. 'Few in industry', the report says, 'believe that the way the financial institutions operate has deprived firms of funds they should have had . . .' In its final report, the committee said: 'We are not opposed on grounds of principle to greater involvement by the public sector as a way of helping to ease the financial problems we have described. But we do not believe that the nationalisation of existing banking or insurance institutions would be helpful.' (Para. 1365). The report goes on to point out that the major constraints on firms' investment are the low level of demand, poor productivity and inadequate profitability considering the cost of capital equipment: all problems which 'nationalisation by itself would do little to help'.

At the same time the committee did not believe the British banking and financial system to be ideal either. During the late 1960s and the 1970s three forces in particular have combined to produce a radically different operating environment from that prevailing in the early 1960s. Continuing inflation at a high level, rapid growth of all types of financial institution, and a steady decline in Britain's industrial performance compared to that of trading rivals: these called for major adjustments in regulations as well as in the attitudes and practices of the institutions.

Since the Wilson Committee reported there have been a number of highly publicised scandals in the City, which have shown clearly the inadequacy of existing regulatory procedures. Additionally, the rate of change of technology has exceeded the wildest dreams of the mid 1970s, opening up new business possibilities and forcing a radical rethink about the type of institution needed to cope in the new environment.

One area in which this rethinking has reached an advanced stage is the whole question of investor protection, which has been the subject of a special enquiry by Professor Lawrence Gower. In his report he recommended the retention of the principle of self-regulation, but within a statutory framework supervised by the Department of Trade and Industry.

Subsequently, the Government announced that it would create two 'self-regulatory bodies', one for the securities, investment and futures industries, and one for life insurance policies and unit trusts. Each of these bodies would have extensive statutory powers to register the various City agencies coming under its authority, to draw up its rules of conduct and to suspend agencies or discipline them in other ways if necessary.

These measures are a consequence of the wide-ranging changes now taking place in many institutions. It is certain that the City of the 1990s will be a very different place as a result.

Besides being the biggest borrower and the ultimate controller, the Government is, of course, involved in many other areas of City life, and in all these it customarily uses the Bank of England as its agent. We shall therefore begin our detailed study of what goes on in the City by looking at this institution.

2 The Bank of England

Emerging from Bank Underground Station beside the Royal Exchange, one is confronted by a massive stone wall, windowless to the second storey, which runs for more than a hundred yards along the north side of Threadneedle Street. This is the Bank of England. The present building extends upwards some seven floors and downwards for a further three; it was designed by Sir Herbert Baker and constructed between 1925 and 1939. Everything about it is impressive. On passing through the massive brass doors one is greeted by large gatekeepers, whose appearance is rendered almost gigantic by the addition of top hats. Their turnout is immaculate, from the gold braid of their top hats down through their pink morning coats to their shining black shoes.

The hall into which the doors admit one is wide and tall and deep, and into its marble floor are set designs in mosaic. At the back of the hall are windows looking out on to a little garden courtyard. Immediately across the courtyard on the ground floor are the offices of the Governor and of the Deputy Governor, and of their secretaries. Above these, in the middle, is the Court Room itself, where the Court of the Bank have their meetings like the Board of Directors of ordinary companies.

Among its more unexpected possessions, the Bank boasts a very fine Roman mosaic, excavated during the construction of the building, and several artesian wells supplying it with fresh water.

The elegant Court Room, where meetings of the Court of the Bank are held

The Bank is very traditional: every evening since the Gordon Riots in 1780 until as recently as 1973, a detachment of Guardsmen was stationed in the building for the night. They were known as the Bank Piquet and for 180 years were a familiar sight marching

The Bank of England, much of which was rebuilt between the wars

through the afternoon traffic to take up their post. Latterly they came by vehicle.

The immensity and splendour of the Bank of England building should, perhaps, convey two things to the visitor. Firstly, of course, it commemorates a very glorious past. The Bank became by far the most important financial institution in the British Empire at the height of British world power. Naturally, the 'Old Lady of Threadneedle Street', as the bank was commonly known then, became extremely wealthy and prestigious. Having an institution of this sort at its head was very important to the British banking system because it instilled confidence and trust into all who had business with Britain. All banks in the nineteenth century issued paper money or notes which could be exchanged for gold if the holder wanted but were meanwhile a more handy form in which to hold money. In order to lend money, banks were in the habit of issuing more notes without having the gold to match them. It was normally a safe procedure, but, then as now, it all depended on public confidence. From time to time situations occurred which caused this confidence to falter. For example, in 1866 Overend, Gurney & Co., a bank prominent in bill discounting, had too many 'doubtful' bills in its possession and was ruined by debtors defaulting. In 1890 Barings, a very sound bank, was badly shaken when an issue of stock which it was selling to the public was not bought: at the time the bank had not sufficient liquid funds with which to honour its obligations to purchase the stock itself. In both these cases, the Bank of England cut short the ensuing public panic by lending widely in order to prevent the crisis from spreading.

The second fact that the visitor to the Bank should be reminded of by its imposing size is its place in the world today. It is the foremost central bank, and the leading institution in the City which is still the greatest market-place in the world. Since the nineteenth century, the Bank has shouldered many responsibilities. Nationalisation in 1946 did not initiate Government control in the City: it merely formalised the existing situation. The Bank and the Treasury had long been working together but by the Act of 1946 final control was vested in the Government and the statutory rights of the Bank over policy were restricted to that of giving advice. As Professor Sayers has put it, 'in short, the "Old Lady of Threadneedle Street" retains her right to nag'.[1]

In keeping with the national significance of the Bank of England, its Governor is appointed by the Crown, which in practice means the Prime Minister. Normally, he would be a man already prominent elsewhere in the City. Lord O'Brien, who retired in 1973, was a recent, rare, example of a man who has worked his way up through the Bank. The present Governor, Mr Robin Leigh-Pemberton, was previously Chairman of National Westminster Bank. The Governor is responsible for the overall running of the Bank and has a Court of Directors to assist him.

Of the eighteen members of the Court, only four besides the

1. Sayers: *Modern Banking* (sixth edition). p. 71.

Governor and the Deputy Governor are full-time or 'executive' Directors. The rest are part-time or non-executive Directors and their function is to advise the others, drawing on the breadth of their experience in a wide variety of careers, e.g. banking, industry, trade unions and the universities.

The Court normally meets once a week on Thursdays. In between these meetings there are various standing committees meeting, of which the chief is the Committee of Treasury. This has seven members, including the Governor, who presides over it, and the Deputy Governor; its job is to advise on important issues of Bank policy.

The functions of the Bank

Managing the Government's debt

As we said earlier, the reason for which the Bank was founded in 1694 was to look after the Government's debt, commonly called the National Debt, and this is still a most important function. The debt is managed from 'New Change', the Bank's extension building a little over a quarter of a mile to the west of the main building and right beside St Paul's. Here there are 800 people employed in registering annually over 1 million transfers of stock and in sending out almost 5 million interest payments – a far cry from the seventeen clerks required to manage the original loan of £1.2 million! The total volume of the Government's debt has now reached almost £143,000 million, and is steadily growing. Many people, alarmed by the sheer enormity of the sum, have given money or bequeathed legacies in their wills to help pay it off. But in fact the Government has no desire to see it paid off, and we should perhaps look at why it takes this view. The answer is that most of the debt is owed to people within the country and therefore interest payments are merely transfers from the community as a whole to sections of it. The money goes round the country, but not out of it, except for the interest on the fraction of debt actually owed to foreigners.

On the other hand, the Government is anxious to contain the *rate of growth* of the debt, because otherwise taxation has to be raised to pay the rising interest charges, and that is a burden which taxpayers understandably resent.

A large proportion of the debt is made up of Government bonds, that is pieces of paper stating that the holder has subscribed such-and-such a sum of money and is entitled to so much interest per year. Two world wars have helped to swell the issue of bonds to some £90,000 million. But it must not be thought that the Government debt rises only in wartime. Since 1976 alone, a further £50,000 million has been added to the amount outstanding. Another sizeable slice of debt is in the form of Treasury bills, which are rather like post-dated cheques sold by the Government for slightly less than their face value. Their purpose is to provide the Government with day-to-day money to cover the inevitable gaps which occur between its disbursements, e.g. on such things as unemployment benefit, and its receipts from taxation. A third type of debt is the group of National Savings Securities, of which ordinary Post Office (now National Savings Bank) accounts, Savings Certificates and Premium Bonds are perhaps the best-known examples.

The note issue

The Bank of England is the ultimate source from which the general public can obtain cash. Other English banks used to issue their own notes, but now they all use Bank of England notes. Scottish banks have continued to issue their own, but it is an expensive undertaking, and is closely controlled by the central bank in England.

The Bank has its own printing works, at which some 5 million notes are produced daily and a slightly lesser number have to be checked and destroyed. Coins are struck at the Royal Mint. Notes and coins are distributed through the clearing banks, each of which maintains an account at the Bank of England: the banks merely withdraw cash from their accounts as they require it. No attempt is

Banknotes being produced at the Bank's printing works

made by the authorities to control the amount of money in notes that the public holds, but they do try to encourage people to use the larger denominations in the interests of economy. The average life of a £1 note was about nine or ten months, making it much more costly to supply than the £1 coin which has replaced it.

Banker to the Government

This is a slightly different job from managing the Government's debts. The Bank also looks after the bank account of the Government just like an ordinary bank does for its customers. Into this account go all tax receipts and any other transfers of money from the various banks, and out of it go all payments.

Bankers' bank

Because all the important institutions in the City maintain accounts at the Bank, transfers of money between them and the Government, which go on every day, are made very easily. The Bank merely debits one account and credits another. The Bank also holds accounts for important international institutions like the World Bank, for just over a hundred central banks and also for some ordinary foreign banks, making a total of nearly 200 accounts.

24

Managing the Exchange Equalisation Account

The Exchange Equalisation Account is the name of the fund in which are held the gold and foreign currency reserves of the country. The managers of the fund have the task of intervening, from time to time, in the otherwise free market for foreign currency, so as to influence the price of the pound in line with Government policy, or simply to try to maintain a reasonably orderly market.

International responsibilities

The pound is not the only currency whose price has to be carefully monitored and sometimes controlled. Most of the major world currencies have the same problems, and all greatly benefit from international co-operation. Dealing with other central banks and managing money on an international scale has become an important side of the Bank's work. Every month the Governor flies to Basle to spend a weekend in conference with his opposite numbers from the central banks of the other western industrial countries.

Controlling the monetary system of the United Kingdom

The twin aims of the Bank's controlling activity in the City are regulation of institutions and implementation of policy. On the one hand, the Bank stands above and apart from the system, ensuring that standards of honesty and efficiency are maintained by adherence to established rules and procedures. And, on the other hand, the Bank operates within the system as an integral part of it, influencing its dealings in line with current government policy.

Regulation of City institutions

The evolution of the British financial system over centuries has produced an extremely complex pattern of highly specialised organisations, and general regulations are by no means easy to formulate or apply. Of course there are statutes covering very broad areas, like deposit taking which is dealt with in the Banking Act, 1979. There are also some very specific statutes, like the Lloyd's Acts of 1871 and 1982, which apply only to the one Corporation. Many institutions and groups of institutions, though, are largely self-regulating. But no matter what arrangements are in operation, the Bank of England has a keen interest, if not always a statutory obligation, in ensuring that rules and procedures are working as they were intended and that they are sufficient. In this supervisory role the Bank will liaise closely with other City controlling bodies, some of which it helped to establish, such as the

Eighteenth-century cartoon, in which the Bank is depicted as 'The Old Lady of Threadneedle Street'

Take-over Panel (1968) and the Council for the Securities Industry (1978).

A good example of how self-regulation and Bank supervision are combined is provided by the arrangements being formulated for ensuring adequate bank liquidity. The Bank of England regards it as primarily the responsibility of the individual bank's management to keep sufficient liquid assets to be able to meet liabilities (e.g. withdrawals of cash by customers) as they fall due. The Bank has therefore not imposed a set 'prudential ratio', i.e. an across-the-board ratio of liquid assets to liabilities which a bank has to keep to meet withdrawals of funds, but it monitors banks' liquidity, taking account of their particular characteristics, type of business, etc. (Further details of the Bank's supervision of the banking system are discussed on p. 43.)

Implementation of policy

For some years now the Government has emphasised the importance of reducing the rate of inflation by following appropriate monetary policies. Since 1976, formal targets have been set for the rate of growth of one or more of the various measures of money supply. The Bank operates in a number of areas in support of the Government's overall strategy. In addition, the Bank has concern for the stability of the main financial markets in the United Kingdom and for the development of competition between different institutions on broadly equal terms.

The Bank has a variety of instruments at its disposal to support the Government's monetary policy. In particular, are the following:

1. Open market operations. This is the name given to the activities of the Bank in the financial markets for control purposes. Of course, the Bank is active in those markets all the time, either as an agent for the Government or simply in its job of day-to-day supervision. The point is that, by its intervention, the Bank can influence markets to move in the direction it desires.

(a) The Bank can influence the level of *short-term interest rates*

27

through operating in the money markets. These operations are primarily conducted in certain types of bills of exchange and mainly with money market specialists known as discount houses. The terms on which the Bank is prepared to conduct business influence short-term interest rates. These in turn affect, for example, bank base rates, mortgage rates and the money supply.

(b) The Bank can also affect the money supply by its operations in the *gilt-edged market*, where it buys and sells Government debt (much of it long-term). Other things being equal, sales of gilt-edged by the Bank lead to the private sector (i.e. companies and private individuals) reducing its holdings of money (as it pays for the gilt-edged it has bought).

2. Suggestion and request. From time to time the Bank will make suggestions to the other institutions in the City, indicating the policy the authorities intend to pursue. If it wants specific action, the Bank issues requests.

3. Special deposits. From time to time the Government may wish to reduce the amount of money that people can borrow in order to reduce the amount they spend. An effective way of doing this is to reduce what the banks have available for lending, and this is done by requiring them to deposit more money at the Bank of England in special accounts from which it cannot be withdrawn until the Bank says so. For any bank, the size of these special deposits is given as a percentage of the deposits which the general public has made at that bank.

3 The discount houses and the money market

Dotted about the City, but mostly close to the Bank of England, are the nine discount houses. These institutions make their living by borrowing money from those who have it to spare and investing it in various easily liquidated paper assets. Among other things, they help to finance the Government by buying some or all of its Treasury bills each week. Before *Competition and Credit Control* (1971), and the changes associated with that document, the houses used to meet first and decide between themselves on a joint bid for all the Treasury bills on offer that week. This is still done: but they now compete both among themselves and with outsiders, that is companies or wealthy individuals with cash to spare for a few months. The houses still collectively underwrite the whole offer of Treasury bills each week, each house in proportion to its size, to ensure that the Government's financing needs will always be met. In return for this useful service, the Bank of England acts as 'lender of last resort' to the houses to provide them with cash when they can't obtain it elsewhere. Such assistance may be given either in the form of outright loans or by means of cash purchases of paper assets from the houses. The interest rate charged for such assistance is known as the Bank's Intervention Rate.

To understand the role of lender of last resort it is necessary first to appreciate the extremely delicate nature of the discount houses'

Main entrance hall of the offices of the Union Discount Company of London Ltd – a prominent discount house

business. Practically all the money which they lend has itself been lent to them. What is more, most of it will have been lent to them for very short periods of time, typically overnight but sometimes for up to a week, or else it will be subject to recall at very short notice. Using this sort of money, the houses buy bills, CDs (Certificates of Deposit) and even bonds in the open market, some of which might not be repurchased or 'redeemed' from them for months. This practice is known as 'borrowing short and lending long' and can be hazardous. Should those who have lent to the houses decide to recall their money, the houses might have some difficulty in getting it back in a hurry. On any given day, each house will find some of its assets maturing and therefore being redeemed for cash and it may also sell assets in the market. At the same time, it will also receive new loans. But it quite often happens that the proceeds of these transactions are insufficient to provide for the calls that are made by those who have lent to the house. It is then that they turn to the Bank of England as lender of last resort.

The chief sources of cash for the discount houses – collectively known as the discount market – are the banks, the building societies and ordinary companies which find themselves with cash to spare. Prudence dictates that all financial institutions should hold a certain proportion of the money deposited with them by the general public in liquid form, that is in the form of cash or some other asset that can be turned into cash quickly and without losing its value. For example, a building is not a liquid asset because it takes time to sell: a quick sale can only be achieved if the owner is prepared to see it go at a knock-down price. Loans to the discount market are therefore ideal assets from the banks' point of view. In fact, all eligible banks are required to keep a certain proportion of their 'eligible liabilities' (roughly, customers' deposits) in this form and many other banks and licensed deposit-takers also choose to keep money with the discount market. Such loans can be at an agreed rate for an agreed period, in which case the houses call them 'fixtures', or they can be simply 'at call', again at an agreed rate but one which will vary as market conditions change. Loans 'at call' can be withdrawn whenever the lender needs them.

An important part of the job of the money manager in a discount house is to make sure that he has the right balance between fixtures and call money. If there is a general trend in the market for rates of interest to rise so that borrowers have to pay more this week than last and will have to pay more next week than this, it is in the interests of the house to persuade institutions to lend to it for fixed periods. Otherwise call money will be quickly withdrawn and offered back to them again at a higher rate! Similarly, when the rate in the market is rising, the houses themselves take care not to make too many long-term loans, the rate of interest on which will soon fall below the general market rate. The houses that can best judge which way things will go make the greatest profits.

Almost all the loans that are made by banks to the discount market are secured. This simply means that the lender requires the houses to which he is lending to place in his keeping assets of equivalent or, more usually, greater value than the loan. This security or collateral, as it is sometimes called, takes the form of a parcel of different bills, CDs and bonds which, together, have the requisite face value. It is returnable when the loan is repaid.

The institutions which borrow from the discount houses fall into three categories: the Government, the local authorities and industry. These three raise funds from the sale of Treasury bills, local authority bills and bills of exchange, respectively, to the discount market.

A typical day

Every house runs a money book, in which all its transactions are entered day by day. Not very long ago this was kept by hand in a large ledger, but now it is done by computer. The money dealer sits surrounded by telephones and VDUs. One of the VDUs displays the current state of the money book, listing the day's receipts and payments and calculating the house's borrowing need minute by minute.

By the end of any day a house's opening position for the next day will be on the screen, having been prepared by the computer from the information stored in its files. Already listed, therefore, would be the receipts that the house will receive from assets due to mature and payments resulting from the fixtures falling due that day. The subtraction of receipts from payments gives the first borrowing requirement of the day.

What happens next depends entirely on what the market is doing, as we discussed earlier. More than likely, however, quite a sizeable amount of money could be required initially as several calls are made on the house. Also, it is likely that those with money to lend and a whole day ahead of them will start by asking quite a high price for it. A money manager with a cool head will wait if he thinks that a potential lender will be more amenable to lower offers towards the end of the day. Indeed, if he thinks there will be plenty of money about later in the day which can be borrowed cheaply, the manager will buy additional assets early, which, of course, increases the house's borrowing requirement. The price of misjudging the market and finding oneself with a requirement still to cover near the

32

A busy dealing room, where the discount house's transactions are made and recorded

end of the day is having to borrow in the market or from the Bank of England at a rate a good deal higher than the ones that were refused earlier in the day, or having to sell bills back to the Bank at an unprofitable rate!

During the day the discount house's agents, recognisable at once by their top hats, may well be out on foot visiting banks and other institutions in person to enquire after business. The main object of such visits is not really to borrow money, as most of that is done over the telephone. Their purpose is to maintain the personal contacts which are such an important feature of the way the City operates.

How a bill works

Earlier we said that a bill was a sort of post-dated cheque issued by someone who needed to borrow money for a few months. That is all right as far as it goes, but now we must be more specific. A

Treasury bill is simply an undertaking by the Government to repay a straight loan at a given date. The certificates used are of different colours, depending on the denomination of the loan, to reduce the risk of muddling one for £25,000 with one for £250,000. Every week on a Friday the Government offers these bills for sale by tender, which means that the interested parties must put in sealed bids for the amount they require. The bids are opened and the allocation is made according to the highest bidders, but always at less than the face value of the bills, or at a 'discount' as it is called. As these loans are of such short duration, it is not possible for the borrower to have the name and address of the lender so that the interest due on the loan can be sent by cheque at an agreed time. This would complicate things a lot, especially as the bill could change hands several times in its brief life, and that would greatly reduce its attractiveness. For these reasons, the interest is paid as a discount deducted from the face value of the bill every time it is sold. The rate of discount is always quoted in annual terms, so a 12 per cent bill of three months' duration would be discounted when new at 3 per cent off face value or £97 per £100 face value. What if the same bill were to be resold after one month? Very simple. That would mean that there were two months or one-sixth of a year to run. If, in a full year, it would earn 12 per cent, then in one-sixth of a year it would earn one-sixth of 12 per cent, which is 2 per cent. The new price would therefore be £98 per £100.

Local authority bills work in a similar way, but commercial bills of exchange are slightly different because in their case they are not only drawn by one party on someone else who is ultimately going to repay the loan, but there is also a transaction in goods involved at the same time. This sort of bill is really an order to someone to pay up what they owe. For example, if Smith the Timber Merchant sells wood to Jones the Joiner, then Jones owes Smith money. Now it quite often happens that, while the seller needs his money at once, the buyer cannot afford to pay him until he has had time to process the goods. In our example, Smith requires payment but Jones needs time to make something out of the wood and sell it. To get his

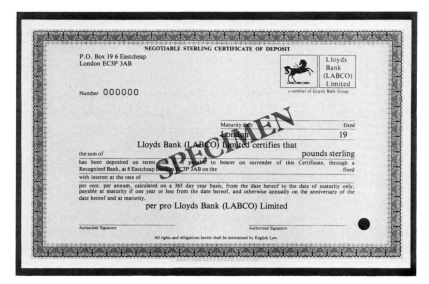

A negotiable Certificate of Deposit

money, Smith draws a bill on Jones who is called the drawee; that is, Smith sends Jones a bill requiring him to pay the full amount owing at a certain date in the future. By signing it, Jones accepts his liability to pay and then a third party may be willing to buy the bill from Smith, at a discount. Smith would then have the money and Jones would have the time he required to process his wood. Discount houses specialise in being third parties to this kind of transaction. Many commercial bills are underwritten, i.e. guaranteed, by banks. The role of the bank here is known as accepting. It makes the bill much safer because the discount house knows that, even if Jones falls off the roof of the house he is building, the bank is sound and will pay up at the agreed time.

Many large companies are able to negotiate 'acceptance credit facilities' with their banks, whereby they are permitted to draw bills directly on the bank, up to an agreed sum. This is the cheapest form of borrowing available to firms, but it cannot be used to finance the purchase of fixed assets, only stock-in-trade.

The assets of the discount houses

The reader will realise by now that the houses have to be very careful about what sort of assets they hold, and how many of each. Bills drawn on companies which are not well known will tend to earn more than bills drawn on companies whose names are household words, because the degree of risk involved is deemed to be higher. However, some of these more profitable bills may not be acceptable to other institutions as security for further loans to the houses. The exact balance between bonds, bills and other assets varies from day to day.

The other major paper asset of the houses is the negotiable Certificate of Deposit, or CD, which has already been mentioned. This sounds more complicated than it really is. The CD was invented during the 1960s and is merely 'a receipt for money deposited with a bank, stating the agreed terms and including an undertaking to repay the amount with any interest outstanding at a fixed date to the bearer'.[1] Its purpose is to encourage companies to make large deposits at banks for long periods of time (generally between three months and one year). The banks can then be more sure of their money when making loans, but the depositor does not lose control of his money because he can always resell the certificate to someone else (i.e. it is negotiable). The minimum deposit is £50,000 and can be for any value above that in multiples of £10,000.

Are discount houses really necessary?

'It would not be beyond human ingenuity to replace the work of the discount houses, but they are there, they are doing the work effectively and they are doing it at a trifling cost in terms of labour and other real resources.' So said the *Radcliffe Report*, published in 1959, in answer to the question which is most often asked of these unique British institutions. They do not exist anywhere else, so why do we have them? The fact is that those who work with them

1. From *Negotiable Sterling Certificates of Deposit* by the Union Discount Co. of London Ltd.

prefer to keep them. They are specialists who save others unnecessary labour.

The Bank of England, in particular, finds the discount houses very useful. It looks on them as a kind of 'buffer' between itself and the rest of the financial system. Through constant close contact with these nine institutions the bank is effectively simultaneously in touch with the 400 or so banks with which the houses are dealing. Secondly, the houses provide the banks with somewhere to keep their cash, a place from where it can be withdrawn instantly should the need arise but where, meanwhile, the money earns interest. This is a valued source of security and stability for the whole financial system. Thirdly, as noted at the start of this chapter, the houses collectively cover the Treasury bill tender week by week.

It is in recognition of their services and of their key role in helping the Bank of England to manage the daily flows of money that the Bank acts as lender of last resort to the discount houses. Of course, the services of the houses could be provided in some other way, for example within the Bank of England itself. But this just emphasises the truth that there is a job to be done. Granted that, there is always going to be room to argue over who could do it best.

4 The clearing banks

A very short walk from the Bank of England in a southerly direction brings one to the top end of Lombard Street. The original Lombards were Italian money-lenders who settled there during the thirteenth and fourteenth centuries in order to be close to the merchants whose trade they were helping to finance. The street is now the home of many of the great banks. The best known are the 'big four' clearing banks, Barclays, Lloyds, Midland and National Westminster. However, there is no direct connection between the old occupants of the street and the present ones, because the Lombards were only money-lenders and not bankers; they did not accept deposits of other people's money, but only lent what they already possessed.

Our modern banks are descendants of the gold and silversmiths of old. These were the people who were properly equipped for looking after valuables because, of course, they had to guard their stock-in-trade carefully; so, in days when the only form of money was precious metal, the services of the smiths were much in demand. Gold, for all its uses, presented some very real problems to its owner, as it still does today. Firstly, it is incredibly heavy stuff to move about, and secondly, there is the risk of theft. So the practice grew up among goldsmiths of taking in other people's gold for safe keeping and issuing an IOU in exchange. With this piece of paper the owner could always redeem his gold, less an appropriate fee, of course. In time, as the goldsmith's reputation for honesty spread, the owners of the gold would find that the IOU itself was acceptable in payment for goods and services. If the IOU were larger than the debt, then instead of handing it over, a man would write a note to his goldsmith requesting him to give to the bearer of that note the requisite sum in gold. This, too, was perfectly acceptable.

Thus there grew up what we know today as the banknote and the cheque, respectively. The only note we have in England now is the Bank of England note, but the words of the IOU are still there: the

Two cheques dating from the nineteenth century and issued by a bank later absorbed into Lloyds

Bank 'promises to pay the bearer' whatever the sum is. A cheque is an order to your bank to pay some person specified by you, and it is authorised by your signature. Every bank supplies its customers with printed forms for this purpose now, but the principle is exactly the same today as it was centuries ago.

Of course, there is one important respect in which the old IOU differs from the modern banknote, and that is in the matter of convertibility. The goldsmith would give £1 worth of gold for a £1 IOU: the Bank of England will not, but it used to do so. The right of the ordinary man to demand payment in gold was only finally abolished in 1931. Internationally, the pound is freely convertible into other currencies.

Nearly all banks in Britain today are what are known as joint-stock banks. That means that they are owned jointly by members of the general public who hold shares in them, as are many other public companies. But not all banks are clearing banks. This name is reserved for the members of the London Bankers' Clearing House. Besides the Bank of England, these are the 'big four' plus other British banks like Coutts, the Trustee Savings Bank, the National Girobank and the Co-operative Bank. The Clearing House is in Post Office Court, at the top end of Lombard Street, and its affairs are in the hands of a Committee of London and Scottish Bankers on which sit representatives of member banks.

The purpose of the Clearing House is to facilitate the transfer of funds between banks in order to settle debts which arise in the normal course of business. For example, when goods and services are paid for by cheque, the recipient pays the cheque into his own bank. But that piece of paper has to find its way back to the branch of the bank on which it was drawn if it is to be paid. So, the cheque has to be physically transferred from one bank to the other, and that is organised by the Clearing House. Every day, over six million cheques, worth an average of £27,000 million, are exchanged between member banks and any differences are settled by the payment of a cheque drawn on the debtor's account at the Bank of England.

THE CLEARING HOUSE.
1902

An Edwardian print of the Clearing House, Post Office Court

Increasingly, money transfer is taking place electronically and soon such facilities will be available to everyone. This development, together with demands for membership of the payment clearing system by outsiders, has led to a thorough review of the present arrangements. Like almost everywhere else in the City, an extensive reorganisation is now in progress.

The essence of High Street banking

The clearing banks are sometimes referred to as the High Street banks to distinguish them from the merchant and other deposit-accepting banks. The title draws attention to the close contact of these banks with the general public, which is certainly one of their distinctive features. By means of a network of thousands of branches – Lloyds Bank, for example, has nearly 2,300 branches – these banks provide a comprehensive service throughout the country. The 'essence' of banking, as we have seen, is the business of bringing lenders and borrowers together, and transferring money on behalf of customers as they direct. Numerous branches are vital for this type of work, but those branches need co-ordination and that is the job of the regional offices, which are themselves co-ordinated by head office back in the City. Another major part of head office's job is managing the funds that are deposited at the branches throughout the country.

A clearing bank's assets

When people make deposits at their bank, the money can be put in a deposit account, a savings account or in a current account. The idea of the deposit account is that the money is expected to be there for some time, and the bank pays interest on it. Nominally, the bank requires seven days' notice before deposits are removed. However, this is normally waived for the ordinary customer so that he may remove his money at any time, but, if so, he forgoes seven days' interest on it. What he may not do, though, is write cheques against money in his deposit account: that is what the current account is for. In the past the Banks have paid no interest on money in current accounts but allowed customers to withdraw it or to transfer it whenever they like by cheque. However, this is changing and some banks are now offering interest subject to minimum deposit requirements.

At a very early stage in banking, the goldsmiths made an important discovery, namely that all their customers did not come on the same day and draw all their money out at once. Indeed, those that did call for their money were often balanced or even outweighed by those who made new deposits. There was no need therefore to keep it all idle in their vaults: a proportion could be lent out quite safely. Today the banks keep only 3 or 4 per cent of the money that has been deposited with them actually on the premises. They have found that margin to be quite sufficient for normal purposes, excepting Christmas time when they stock up a bit more. To be absolutely safe the banks keep a further proportion of their deposits in certain liquid assets, which can be redeemed quickly without loss. As we saw earlier (page 27), the exact size of this 'prudential ratio' depends on the circumstances of each individual bank, subject to each bank's management being able to satisfy the Bank of England that adequate liquidity is available.

In addition to the money the clearing banks keep in their 'current' accounts at the Bank, they have to deposit cash amounting to $\frac{1}{2}$ per cent of their eligible liabilities. This requirement applies to all recognised banks and licensed deposit-taking institutions with eligible liabilities of more than £10 million. It is not connected with monetary policy, but the interest which the Bank of England can earn on these deposits goes towards meeting its running costs.

After having fulfilled its obligations to the Bank of England, it is up to each bank to decide in what form it will hold its money. The guiding principle is this: the more liquid the asset, the safer it is and the less it earns. A bond which is going to be redeemed by the Bank of England in twenty-five years' time is much more risky than a Treasury bill that will be repurchased in one month. There could be a calamity next year that would make all bond prices fall heavily just when the holder needed to sell his bonds, and that would mean a big loss. Meanwhile, the bond will earn more than the bill. Cash, of course, is the most liquid asset of all, but it earns nothing. Indeed, in times of rising prices, people holding their wealth in cash are actually losing money. Loans to the public, on the other hand, pay the banks well because people are prepared to pay high rates of interest. However, the risks are greater than with bonds because individuals are more likely to go bankrupt and be unable to pay

43

their debt than the Government. So, like the discount houses, banks have to weigh up many factors in deciding how to manage their money.

Functions of the clearing banks

Holding money and transferring it

All the clearing banks provide an enormous array of services for their customers. The deposit and current accounts, and the transfer of money by cheque, are all that many customers are aware of: however, these are but the tip of the iceberg. For example, the banks provide machines in some places which dispense cash automatically, on production of a card and a code number, so that their customers can obtain money from their accounts at times when the bank is not open. This service is a very valuable step forward for those customers unable to get to their bank during the banking hours of 9.30 a.m. to 3.30 p.m.

Another type of card is now in general use – the bank credit card. This service was pioneered by Barclays, who run the 'Barclaycard'

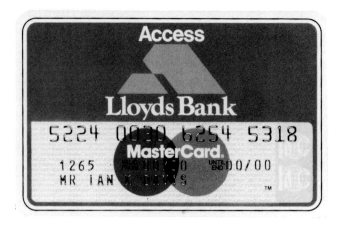

The 'Access' credit card

system, and in 1972 the other three big banks co-operated to establish the rival 'Access' card. The idea is that instead of paying cash at once a customer produces his credit card and signs for the goods. The details of the purchase and of the customer's credit card number are recorded on the form he has signed: one copy is given to the customer. As soon as the credit card company receives notice of the transaction from the seller, it pays the bill on behalf of the purchaser, less a discount of between 2 and 5 per cent of the sale price. The seller is prepared to allow this discount in exchange not only for a quick payment and for being relieved of the need to worry about collecting debts, but also in the belief that accepting the card increases his overall sales. The credit company collects the full value of the goods from the buyer, charging interest on any sum outstanding after a stated time has elapsed since the purchase. In this way the buyer can if he wishes settle the entire bill when he receives it from the credit card company or simply make the minimum repayment required and take advantage of the credit facilities available for the balance outstanding.

Apart from the various 'card' services and the cheque system, the banks also operate a bank 'giro' for paying bills. By filling in the appropriate form, one for each bill, and handing them together with a cheque for the total to one's own bank, one can have all one's bills paid at once, thus saving time, postage and bank charges. Using the same system, an employer can have the wages of all his employees paid automatically into their accounts and avoid the risk of theft.

Children and young people are encouraged to save by means of a savings account, into which very small sums can be paid, and some banks even provide a money box, too.

Budget and Cashflow accounts

Another device for taking the worry out of paying bills is the budget account. The large household bills for items like gas, electricity and the rates and 'hardy annuals' like car tax come in at irregular intervals; unless carefully budgeted for, they cause hiccups in one's personal finances which can be tiresome. The budget account is designed to ease such payments. The customer pays into his account each month one-twelfth of his total annual commitment, and can draw cheques on it to meet the specified bills as and when they fall due even though they may cause an overdraft. In this way the disruption caused by large irregular payments is avoided and the customer is enabled to plan his financial affairs in a systematic way.

Sometimes, unexpected bills come in which cannot be budgeted for, or one suddenly sees a bargain in a sale that one cannot quite afford just then. A new type of chequing account, called a Cashflow account, is designed to take care of this problem. The customer pays in an agreed monthly sum and receives interest on his credit balance. Then, when he needs money quickly, he is entitled to overdraw the account by up to 30 times his monthly payment, up to a ceiling of £5,000.

Lending money

Lending money is the most profitable of a bank's activities but, as we saw earlier, considerations of profitability have to be balanced against risk and liquidity. At present, rather more than half of the clearing banks' total assets are advances to the public.

These advances may be grouped into two types, the overdraft and the loan. The first is really the granting of permission to a customer to overdraw his account up to an agreed ceiling; interest is charged on the amount overdrawn. In the case of a loan, the full agreed sum is credited to the customer's account and repayment dates are set.

Details of interest charges for all advances will be agreed at the outset between the bank's branch manager and the client. The branch manager has a degree of latitude in this but generally speaking the rate is set by the 'base' rate of the bank concerned. All the clearing banks have such a base rate: it is merely a figure in terms of which they fix the rates at which they will borrow from the public through deposit accounts and the rate at which they will

The Foreign Money Section of Lloyds Bank

lend. The banks' lending rates, which normally start at 1 per cent above base rate for their best industrial customers, depend on the credit worthiness of the client and the purpose for which he is borrowing.

Statements, standing orders and custody of valuables

Frequent use of cheques could cause a person to forget how much money he has in his account. To keep him up to date, banks provide their customers with regular statements. They will carry out regular payments, called standing orders, and also, for a small charge, look after non-money valuables like the family silver. Many branches also have night safes, which are receptacles let into the outside wall of the building, into which shopkeepers and such people can post the day's takings in the evenings and be sure they are secure for the night. They can then be paid in or retrieved next day when the bank is open.

Financial advice and financial services

All the clearing banks maintain a staff of experts in many fields to give considered advice to customers on request. The problems they deal with vary from the housewife who has been left £500 in a will and wants to invest it, to the businessman who wants to know how best to go about selling his products in Malaysia. Should the housewife decide to buy some shares in XYZ Company, the bank will handle the transaction for her; and should the businessman want to know the credit worthiness of a Malaysian importer, the bank will find it out for him through the international trade promotion section of its Overseas Department. Apart from these services, one can also list other major roles performed by the clearing banks such as the executorship of wills, investment management including the trusteeship of funds, advice on matters of personal income tax and insurance, and the provision of foreign currency for travel purposes.

Equipment leasing

This is a way of enabling a firm to obtain equipment quickly and cheaply, without having to lay out a large sum of money which it can ill afford. The businessman chooses the equipment he wants and agrees purchase terms with the supplier, but the bank buys it and leases it to him for an agreed period at an agreed rental based on the cost of the equipment.

Services to exporters

The speed of change in the world today is such that the ordinary businessman often finds it difficult or impossible to keep abreast with the regulations and methods of transactions with other parts of the world. The commercial banks provide vital services to overcome these difficulties. Besides having a trained staff whose job it is to keep up to date, they have contacts through a network of correspondent banks abroad which give them access to information on the standing and integrity of individuals and companies. When the client exporter is making arrangements about how he is to receive payment, the banks are again able to give valuable advice and other assistance. Because Britain is so dependent on her trade, export promotion is a very important side of the banks' activities. Exporters can obtain a guarantee from the Government-backed Export Credits Guarantee Department which protects them against the many unforeseeable risks encountered in trading overseas such as the importer being unable to pay for the goods or sudden economic sanctions being imposed by the importing country which prevent normal payment. If exporters have this guarantee then they can obtain finance from the clearing banks at a highly preferential interest rate which is lower than that normally charged even to the best industrial borrowers.

Factoring

Most banks are involved in factoring. The factoring company takes over what are called the 'book debts' of its client company, i.e. the money owing to the company for goods supplied by it, and pays the company a lump sum for them a little below their full book value. The factoring company then supervises the collection of the debts itself. The value of this service is twofold; firstly, it frees the client company from the burden of chasing up its debtors and so enables it to get on with the job for which it really exists, namely the production of goods and services. Secondly, it often helps that company's cash flow in providing cash immediately rather than having to wait for its debtors to pay up.

Costs and competition

The charges for these services vary from bank to bank, and according to the nature of the work. Increasingly sharp competition, particularly from the Building Societies, has had the effect of paring charges down and some have been dropped. Some banks do not charge current accounts, but the guiding principle where charges are concerned is that, if the customer maintains a minimum

A scene in the Computer Operations Section of Lloyds Bank

deposit or average balance above a prescribed level, charges for the use of the account are waived. Even when charges are levied, they are frequently reduced by the now widespread practice of paying interest on all credit balances. Since banks came within the scope of company legislation relating to disclosures of profit and capital figures, they have become very much more conscious of the need to produce better figures than those of their rivals.

Banking is a labour-intensive industry, and in an effort to cut costs as well as to improve efficiency, all the banks have computerised their customers' accounts.

50

5 The merchant banks

Of all the City institutions mentioned in this book, probably the hardest one to define is the merchant bank. There are about fifty companies which by tradition are described as such (though since the Banking Act 1979 only recognised banks – some thirty out of the fifty – have been entitled to call themselves banks); but there is no common link that is the main business of them all. Nor is there a single activity which any of them does which is not also done by some other institution in the City. The oldest of them are descendants of seventeenth- and eighteenth-century merchants who found that the banking and credit side of trade was more profitable than dealing in goods on their own behalf. Barings, for example, had been in the wool trade, and Schroders was in wheat and coffee. Their merchanting links also gave the banks particular interests in certain parts of the world; thus Brown, Shipley were linked with the United States and Hambros with Scandinavia.

The nineteenth century was, in some ways, a 'golden age' of merchant banks. There were fewer of them and, relative to other firms and to governments, they were very large and important. Governments the world over treated them with respect, realising that they might hold the key to the success or failure of great projects for which large sums of money were required. The first Japanese railway line, for example, was financed by a loan raised by Schroders in 1873.

Today, the merchant banks are small compared to the clearing banks, yet the best among them are still household names of the highest repute. Their livelihood depends on maintaining this prestige, for the essence of merchant banking is staking one's reputation. The two types of bank do not really compete: rather, they see their work as complementary. Though merchant banks now offer deposit and cheque book facilities, their function is essentially wholesale rather than retail. Hence, unlike the clearing banks, they do not have recourse to interest-free money on current accounts (though they avoid the enormous expense of running a comprehensive national money transfer service and a branch network). In contrast to the 'mass-production' approach of the High Street banks, the merchant banks prefer to take on fewer transactions; but the average sum involved is much bigger, requiring detailed research and a high degree of expertise. With small executive staffs, often only twenty or less, decisions can be taken quickly and at the most senior level.

The functions of merchant banks

The typical merchant bank has three divisions: banking, corporate finance and investment management. In the interests of customer and investor protection, these divisions are physically and administratively separate; care is taken to maintain 'Chinese walls' between them, to prevent the improper use of confidential, price-sensitive information. The customer nevertheless has the services of all divisions at his disposal; the combined expertise, including that from overseas offices, can be brought to bear to solve his problems. The activities of the merchant banks are described below in three categories: advising, financing and dealing.

Advising

Business under this heading is of three main kinds:
1. *General financial advice.* Many companies retain the services of a merchant bank to give advice from time to time about the general

running of the company; particularly in the area of corporate planning, capital requirements, mergers and take-overs. No shareholding by the bank is involved: the relationship is like that of a doctor giving a patient the occasional check-up. The corporate finance departments of the merchant banks also perform an important function in underwriting the domestic and overseas capital issues of companies and governments which is referred to below.

2. *Take-overs and mergers.* Many merchant bankers are heavily involved in giving advice on this subject. The work comes to them in two main ways. Sometimes firms or individuals approach a merchant bank with a request for help to find a company for them to buy or, alternatively, to find a buyer for their company, or to suggest the terms on which a merger with, or a take-over of another company should be arranged. The merchant banks have access to company data from many sources and can suggest the names of

City merchant bankers and Japanese manufacturers sign a financial agreement

53

possible candidates which might fit the requirements of the client. They can then be researched in greater detail until the list has been whittled down to one to which an approach is made. At this point, another merchant bank will almost certainly become involved because the company which has been approached will need impartial advice even if they favour the proposed merger. This is the second way a merchant bank receives business: it is brought in to advise a client on a situation which has already been set up or to help repel an unwelcome approach by another company. Nor is the bank expected either to rubber-stamp a proposed plan or to lend its name to the rejection of a bid just because it is unwelcome to the Board of the company being bid for: it must be thoroughly checked. Take-overs and mergers in which shareholders' true interests have not been adequately safeguarded have, since the war, attracted some bad publicity, and the City is extremely sensitive on this subject.

A number of important ethical considerations have been raised in the area of take-overs and mergers, and this prompted the Governor of the Bank of England to set up the City Working Party in 1959. This body had representatives from all the leading City institutions like the Accepting Houses Committee and The Stock Exchange. It produced a City code on take-overs and mergers which lays down principles and rules to be followed by all parties. The code is administered by a Panel established by the Working Party: its authority stems not from the law but from the distinction of the City people who are on the Panel and also from the authority of the institutions they represent. To be found in breach of the code is to incur at least a damaging public reprimand, and may also result in the offender's expulsion from whatever City professional association he belongs to. In addition, sanctions may be imposed through The Stock Exchange. The Panel itself, The Stock Exchange and other leading City institutions are now subject to the supervision of a new self-regulatory body called the Council for the Securities Industry.

3. *Investments.* The merchant banks advise on, or manage on a discretionary basis, the investments, property and cash in com-

panies' pension funds and also the portfolios (stock and shareholdings) of private individuals, charities and other customers. In addition, many of them run unit and investment trusts, which derive their funds from public subscription.

Financing

The principal activity under this heading is, of course, the lending of money. It is closely connected to the function of adviser. The merchant banks lend money by providing an acceptance credit facility or on overdrafts or by fixed period loans. Sometimes firms ask the banks to back their advice with money, by buying shares in the company, and even to place a person on the Board to provide continuous expert help. This sort of work is the task of the investment banking section of the merchant bank. Other financing activities are as follows:

1. *Factoring and leasing.* Both these activities were explained in connection with the clearing banks. Once again, they are activities which involve many but not all of the merchant banks.

2. *Property, shipping and foreign trade finance.* To the extent that these involve the banks in ordinary lending business, they are properly included here. The funds to assist exporters tend to be provided chiefly by the clearing banks, but the merchant banks also play an important procuring or managing role.

3. *Accepting.* The 'princes' of merchant banking are the sixteen members of the Accepting Houses Committee. They are the banks for which acceptance business is a major activity. As we saw earlier (page 35), the work involves putting the bank's name to a bill to guarantee payment at the advertised date. Discount houses are then more willing to purchase the bill. In return for staking its reputation in this way the bank receives a commission.

4. *Issuing.* Practically all the merchant banks take some part in issuing new securities for governments, central and local, and industry. The Issuing Houses Association, to which all participants in this work belong, comprises over fifty members. Of course, a great deal of advice and assistance will have gone into the

Working in the foreign exchange dealing room of a leading merchant bank

preparations for a sale of new stocks or shares. As much as two years may pass between the initial approach to a bank by a firm and the eventual issue of its shares, especially if the firm is small and needs some re-organisation prior to its first public issue. The actual job of issuing involves the bank in advertising the security, receiving applications and money, and allotting stock accordingly. In addition, the bank commonly underwrites all or part of the issue, arranging for others to share the burden if necessary. 'Underwriting' in this context means that, if the general public does not buy all of the stock offered for sale, the institution which has underwritten it will buy what is left. It is thus a form of insurance.

Foreign exchange dealing

All merchant banks deal in foreign exchange. This is an important activity for the banks which do a lot of business in international loans of one sort and another.

Bullion

A few banks, led by Rothschilds, manage the London gold market. This is a very specialised interest, which we shall consider later.

Associated activities

Merchant banks are increasingly to be found at the heart of the 'financial conglomerates' being formed in the City. These encompass, within a single group, Stock Exchange firms and other dealers in securities, the management of unit trusts and investment trusts, insurance brokers, life assurance companies, shipping and other interests, with offices in the world's major financial centres.

6 Insurance

The British insurance industry sells its services in over one hundred countries throughout the world. In 1982 this sector of City business earned over £1,170 million from abroad out of the City's total net foreign earnings of over £4,300 million.

Insurance as an activity in Britain goes back at least to the fourteenth century; it was probably introduced by the Lombards whom we met in connection with early money-lending. At this stage, as throughout its history to the present day, insurance would have been closely associated with cargoes and ships, these being large and precious items in any age. It is not surprising, therefore, to find the Baltic Exchange, the commodity markets and the various insurance institutions congregated together in the same quarter of the City now. Today, the City is still a pioneer in insurance, taking credit for being the first to come to terms with some of the truly awesome risks of our day. British insurers were the first, for example, to assess the risks of underwriting nuclear reactors. An 'underwriter' is anyone who accepts a risk by writing his name on an agreement; literally, he writes under (or at the end of) the agreement and so guarantees to fulfil its terms.

When speaking of insurance in Britain, it is customary to distinguish two types of institution: the insurance companies and Lloyd's of London. Both of these institutions do business in both main branches of insurance – life and non-life.

The insurance companies

Although there are some 849 insurance companies operating in the United Kingdom, most of their business is in the hands of about one hundred large companies. The British Insurance Association has a membership of over 340 companies authorised by the Government. These transact between them almost 95 per cent of the business of the British insurance company market. Altogether, in 1983, the companies controlled funds of about £122,650 million and their premium income from sources at home and abroad, which had been growing at an average annual rate of 14.7 per cent since 1978, was close to £24,000 million. Such wealth makes these institutions the foremost investors in industry and in Government stock in the United Kingdom.

Non-life insurance

This class of business covers motor, fire and accident (non-motor), marine, aviation and transport insurance. 'Accident' must be interpreted in the widest sense to include theft and fraud. The companies do over two-thirds of non-life insurance. They have the advantage of a nationwide branch system, and a mass-production type of approach which makes dealing with standard risks a very simple matter.

Apart from marine insurance, fire insurance is probably the oldest branch. It was developed in the City after the great fire in 1666. Nicholas Barbon established the first company and this was at once a success. A natural extension for a fire insurance company in those days was a fire brigade of its own: there was no public fire service like we have today. When a fire was reported, someone would speedily run to the scene and check if the building had the fire insurance company's sign, which all insured houses had pinned in a prominent place on the outside wall. If it was there, the fire brigade would turn out and endeavour to save as much of the property as possible in order to minimise the bill the insurance company would be required to pay. In 1832 several of the companies merged their brigades and then in 1865 the local authority took over the job.

About two-thirds of company non-life insurance premiums come from overseas, especially from the United States. Recently, however, claims from that country have been so heavy that some companies have reduced their business there. Nor is the traffic all one way: about 170 foreign companies are actively engaged in the British market.

Life insurance

Most of the big companies handle life insurance business as well as non-life, and there are altogether about one hundred companies which undertake only life insurance. Many life policies today have a savings scheme attached and the regular instalment paid by the client is often, therefore, two payments rolled together. The first is a straightforward insurance premium, in return for which the company guarantees to pay a certain sum to the insured's dependants should he die suddenly. The second part of the payment en-

Eighteenth-century caricature representing a busy day in a London coffee house

titles the policy-holder to an agreed lump sum should he survive to a certain age.

The life insurance business of today really grew out of the work of Halley, one-time Astronomer Royal, who first calculated a reliable basis for assessing life expectation, although the principle of insuring one's life goes back a good deal further.

Other activities of insurance companies

As professional money managers the insurance companies have for some time been taking on business outside the scope of insurance. They have become managers of pension funds for numerous companies and other institutions, and trustees of unit trusts. They are recognised specialists in the basic activities of investing funds safely and it is obviously cheaper and easier for many firms to pay insurance companies to manage their staff pension scheme than for them to try to do it themselves.

Lloyd's of London

Lloyd's is an incorporated society of private insurers; this status was given to it by Act of Parliament in 1871. However, the collection of underwriters that comprise the Corporation had been in the habit of working together for years before that date. In fact Lloyd's traces its origins back nearly 300 years to a coffee house run by a man called Edward Lloyd, not far from the docks. Lloyd set out to cater for a merchanting clientele: he sent runners to the docks to obtain the latest information on things like arrivals, departures, cargoes and losses. This news was proclaimed by the waiters to the patrons as they drank their beverages and discussed their business. One particular business for which many ship owners, captains and merchants met at Lloyd's was to arrange the insurance of ships and cargoes; for this, accurate, up-to-date information was essential. So successful was Lloyd's service that his coffee house rapidly became *the* place for obtaining shipping insurance in London.

In 1771 the patrons elected a committee to manage the

establishment. Shortly after, they left the coffee house and moved to more suitable premises in the Royal Exchange. In 1811 rules were laid down and a formal constitution was adopted. Since then this constitution has been altered and up-dated as times have changed, but the actual floor where business was conducted did not look all that different from today's floor.

Towards the end of the nineteenth century, Lloyd's, which up to then was primarily a marine insurance market, began to underwrite non-marine business. At first only fire and burglary risks were taken on, but today all classes of insurance, except long-term life and financial guarantee, may be placed at Lloyd's. In 1971, a separate company was set up by the Corporation of Lloyd's to accept long-term life insurance business.

Lloyd's today

The modern Lloyd's is situated in Lime Street. The Underwriting Room, where business is transacted, is 340 feet long by 120 feet wide and slightly crescent-shaped. Pew-like desks, called 'boxes', are set in rows both downstairs and up in the gallery which runs all round the Room.

The total membership of Lloyd's now exceeds 26,000 'names', 80 per cent of whom do not work in the Lloyd's market. These 'external names' must have a personal fortune of at least £100,000 and they must actually deposit a substantial part of this with the Corporation of Lloyd's as security for their underwriting liabilities. The remaining 20 per cent of the membership are 'working names', for whom also the requisite deposit must be made, although their personal wealth need not be as much as for external names. In all cases, the liability of members in the event of claims against risks they have underwritten is unlimited. This fact, together with the increasing size of risks undertaken, has long made it necessary for members to seek safety in numbers and they are now grouped in over 400 'syndicates', each managed by an agent who is responsible for providing the underwriting expertise. These groups of members compete hotly both with one another and with the

The Underwriting Room at Lloyd's, where almost every type of insurance is transacted

insurance companies outside. Some syndicates still have only a few members, but others run to several hundred names and are well able to take business in competition with even the biggest insurance companies.

The syndicates rent 'box' space from the Corporation of Lloyd's according to their size; some may share a box while others require a whole area of boxes. Seated at the boxes are the underwriters and their staffs, who are employed by their syndicate to take on risks on behalf of the whole group, each member accepting liability only for his share of a risk. The part of the Room in which any syndicate is situated depends on its area of interest. Marine, aviation and motor business, i.e. 'transport insurance', is done downstairs, the rest up in the gallery.

The brokers

Members of the public cannot place insurance risks direct with Lloyd's underwriters. Instead, the public must deal through one of some 270 firms of insurance brokers accredited by the Corporation of Lloyd's. Of all the thousands of insurance brokers in the United Kingdom these alone are allowed to style themselves 'Lloyd's brokers' and place business in the Room. Representatives of these firms go on to the floor armed with details of their clients' needs and they search out the best offers from among the underwriters. The main facts of the risk the client wants to be insured against are set out on a piece of paper called a 'slip'. The first thing the broker does is to obtain quotations for the rate of premium from a few leading underwriters. Eventually he chooses an underwriter who has made a reasonable offer and invites him to 'lead' the slip at the agreed premium by signing his name on it and writing in details of their bargain. This signature makes it a binding agreement. After that the broker finds other underwriters to agree to the rest of the risk at the same rate of premium by adding their signatures. Each syndicate that participates will get a share of the premium in proportion to its share of the risk, and will bear a similar proportion of any loss.

When a risk is 100 per cent covered, the broker returns to his office and prepares the policy. This is checked, signed and sealed by a Corporation department, Lloyd's Policy Signing Office, on behalf of the syndicate concerned, and the broker then forwards the policy to his client.

Lloyd's Corporation

The job of the Corporation, which is managed by an elected committee of members, is to provide premises and services for the insurance market. It does not insure risks or incur liability through members' actions, although it does take great care to see that all valid claims will be met whatever the cost to members. It employs about 2,000 staff and rents a large amount of office space to individuals and organisations in the Lloyd's market as well as to

The Lutine Bell, which is rung to obtain silence before important announcements are made

insurance companies. The advantage of having all the competitors close together is that a Lloyd's broker can easily go to the companies as well as to Lloyd's syndicates in search of the best coverage for his client.

Like many City institutions, Lloyd's is in many small ways traditional. The employees of the Corporation working on the floor are called 'waiters' and still wear livery. One of them operates the public address system, which enables a broker to be 'called' on the floor at any time from a rostrum in the centre of the Room. Hanging above the rostrum is the famous Lutine Bell, which came from the frigate *La Lutine*, captured from the French in 1793. As HMS *Lutine*, she was carrying gold and silver bullion in 1799 when she sank in a storm off the Dutch coast at Terschelling. The cargo, worth perhaps £1,400,000, was insured at Lloyd's but in subse-

Reports giving details of marine, aviation and non-marine losses are posted during the day on the Casualty Board

quent attempts to retrieve it only about £100,000 in bullion was raised, together with the bell and other odds and ends. Nowadays, the Lutine Bell is rung only when important announcements are to be made to the market – two strokes for good news and one for bad.

Lloyd's intelligence

If the Bell were rung for every loss at sea, it would, alas, ring rather often, as any reader of the Casualty Book, which stands in the middle of the floor, would see. Every day, somewhere in the world there are total losses and these are recorded in that book. Next to it are the Casualty Boards, on which are pinned sheets of information likely to be relevant to members; yellow sheets for marine news, pink for non-marine and blue for aircraft.

This information comes from many sources. An important one is the world network of 1,300 Lloyd's agents and sub-agents. In addition, Lloyd's of London Press Ltd produces a range of daily and weekly publications for the insurance, shipping and commercial community, including *Lloyd's List*, which is London's oldest daily newspaper, founded in 1734.

Lloyd's in the 1980s

The 1980s see Lloyd's in the throes of great changes. The enormous increase in the membership of the market and in the size and complexity of the risks underwritten has made it necessary to alter and clarify the Society's legal basis which derives from Lloyd's Act of Parliament, 1871. The main provision of the Lloyd's Act, 1982, is the transfer of legislative power from the Society's underwriting members to an elected Council which will also be responsible for operating a more effective disciplinary code than that provided by the original Lloyd's Act.

Apart from constitutional reform, a new Lloyd's building is being constructed on the site of premises in Leadenhall and Lime Streets vacated by Lloyd's in 1958. The present building is 'bursting at the seams': extra space has had to be found by converting the underground car-park and erecting pre-fabricated offices on the roof! The new building is expected to be completed in 1986, just two years short of the three-hundredth anniversary of the opening of Edward Lloyd's coffee house.

7   The Stock Exchange

The Stock Exchange is probably one of the best-known exchanges in this country. Situated in Threadneedle Street, it is in the heart of the square mile, overlooking the Bank of England. As with Lloyd's, the business which now occupies the floor used to be carried on in coffee houses in the seventeenth and eighteenth centuries; and at one time it was also conducted at the Royal Exchange. In 1773, a group of stockbrokers decided to establish their own meeting place and took premises accordingly, but the tradition of referring to attendants as 'waiters' was carried over and continues to the present day. In 1802, the market moved to the site which it has occupied ever since, but the present multi-storey building was only completed in 1973.

Also in 1973, the London Stock Exchange merged with the provincial and Irish exchanges in Glasgow, Liverpool, Manchester, Birmingham, Bristol, Cardiff, Dublin and Belfast. This group is known simply as The Stock Exchange. The main trading floor and the administrative centre is in London. The total membership is now over 4,500 in 211 firms of brokers and seventeen firms of jobbers.

Some 7,000 different securities are quoted in the daily Official List of The Stock Exchange and may therefore be bought and sold on the floor. It is the second-largest stock market in the world, by value of securities quoted. Almost seven-eighths of the total are company issues and the rest are United Kingdom and foreign central and local government stocks.

The function of The Stock Exchange

Strictly speaking no securities are sold directly on to The Stock Exchange by the issuer. Instead, they are sold to individuals or institutions first, who are then free to resell them on the floor of the exchange provided that The Stock Exchange Council have signified their approval by listing the security in their Official List.

The essential function of The Stock Exchange, therefore, is to provide an efficient, centralised market-place for existing securities of any type approved by the Council. The importance of this role lies in the fact that people will only lend money to industry and the Government if they can get it back again when they need it, without a lot of trouble and hopefully without loss. An efficient market is the best guarantee of this. There are now between 3 and 4 million shareholders throughout the country, so the likelihood is very high that someone somewhere will be wanting to sell shares just when someone else is wanting to buy them. It is also a free market, in the sense that no one controls the price of any securities: they move according to the dictates of supply and demand.

Types of security

The types of security dealt in on The Stock Exchange can be divided into three groups:
1. Gilt-edged.
2. Debentures and other loan stock.
3. Preference and ordinary shares.
Gilt-edged is the name given to the bonds issued by Her Majesty's Government of the United Kingdom. The term conveys the impression of reliability which has characterised British Government debt for so long.

Debentures are company-issued loan stocks; and the latter is merely a term for a bond which has not been issued by the United

70

The Stock Exchange Building, completed in 1973, which stands on the site that the Exchange has occupied for nearly two centuries

Kingdom Central Government. So there are, for example, Birmingham Corporation loan stocks, and many other British local authority bonds. Many foreign government stocks and industrial issues are also quoted on The Stock Exchange.

Shares are certificates entitling the holder to participate in the ownership of a company, and to receive its profits if there are any. The 'preference' shareholder is only entitled to a fixed percentage of the profits, but must be paid before the 'ordinary' shareholder. The latter, therefore, runs the risk that little profit may be left to pay him in bad years, though in good years he could receive twice as much as the preference shareholder.

Members of The Stock Exchange

About 80 per cent of the membership are stockbrokers: that means they act on behalf of their clients, the public at large, just like insurance brokers do. The other 20 per cent are jobbers, who are unique to The Stock Exchange in London. They are 'principals', which means they act on their own behalf, buying from and selling to the brokers but not the public. This system of having two types of member is commonly referred to as 'single capacity' trading. In the changes due to be implemented in 1986, the distinction will be removed by a change in the rules to allow firms to act as both brokers and jobbers, i.e. to have 'dual capacity'.

The layout of the floor of the London exchange shows clearly the difference between the two functions. There are hexagonal stands grouped around the room according to sections of the market, and these are occupied by the jobbers. The brokers move about between them.

Finding a broker

The Stock Exchange can supply a list of brokers' names and addresses. Alternatively, one can go to one's bank and receive the same service from there. All the banks are clients of at least one broking firm, through which they carry out their customers' transactions.

A transaction

When people wish to carry out a transaction in shares or bonds, they write to their broker (or bank) with their instructions. If they do not really know what to do for the best, they may, in the first instance, request advice. Suppose that the final decision is to buy some shares in ICI. When the stockbroker's office is informed of this order, they put a call through to their broker on the floor of the exchange and he goes over to the area of the room where the jobbers who specialise in chemicals are situated. On finding one, the broker asks him his price for ICI shares, taking care not to disclose at this stage whether he is a seller or a buyer. The jobber therefore gives two prices, say 668 to 671 pence, a (lower) buying price and a (higher) selling price. A good broker will not accept this price at once, but will go off and see if he can find another, better, offer from a different jobber. When he thinks he has got the best quotation, which in this case means the lowest selling price offered, he accepts it and then discloses that he is a buyer. Both of them then make a quick note of the main details of the bargain in their notebooks – the name of the other party, the stock dealt in, how many shares, at what price and whether bought or sold – and that is all there is to it.

'My word is my bond' is the motto of The Stock Exchange and it is the principle which underlies all trading on the floor. Such a system depends on mutual trust. If people started to deny later the agreements they had made during the day, the whole market would quickly become inoperable. But such is the integrity of the dealers that this does not happen. The result, therefore, is that transactions are very quick and simple to clinch, and much time and expense is saved.

What does it cost?

For his services, the broker charges his client a fee in the form of a commission, the size of which varies according to the value of the transaction and type of security. On sums of £300 or less where ordinary shares are concerned, the rate is at the broker's discretion.

The floor of The Stock Exchange

Between £300 and £424 it is £10 to buy, £7 to sell, and thereafter 1.65 per cent. On Government and other loan stock, the rates are lower for all transactions. In all cases they fall further the larger the sums that are dealt in. Fixed minimum commissions are due to be scrapped by the end of 1986 and this will probably lead to a sharp increase in competition between member firms.

There is also a transfer stamp duty on the purchase of ordinary shares of 1 per cent. Brokers do not normally charge extra for advice but they spend a great deal of money and time in research so that they can give clients good guidance about their shares.

The Stock Exchange Council

The smooth running of this market is the task of The Stock Exchange Council, which has 46 elected members and a further five 'lay' members chosen from outside the industry. This is the body which ensures that the rules are obeyed; any alleged breaches are examined closely, and if any impropriety is established, the Council will take disciplinary action, which could mean the banning of the offender from The Stock Exchange, depending on the nature of the misdemeanour. The task of safeguarding the investing public is taken very seriously.

It is the Council, too, which authorises the admission of new securities to the floor, but only after detailed scrutiny of the affairs of the company concerned. Every effort is made to ensure that the company is genuine in its intentions and is efficiently run. As their approval is so vital to a company seeking a listing or, for that matter, to a company wanting to retain or recover its listing, the Council has great authority in the City.

The Unlisted Securities Market

Meeting the requirements of the Council for a firm to be listed can be quite an expensive business and may be beyond the means of small firms. The Unlisted Securities Market (USM) was established by The Stock Exchange in 1980 with the aim of aiding such companies, with good prospects, to raise money on less onerous terms. In its first three years, the USM provided more than £200 million.

8 Other financial institutions and markets

To assign the rest of the City institutions and markets to a single chapter may seem rather a harsh way to treat, for example, a group of banks whose total deposits exceed £150,000 million, and a market the total turnover of which is thought to approach 400 billion dollars! There are a number of reasons for this approach, however. Chiefly, shortage of space does not permit one to take more than a glance at any but the best-known national institutions in the City. Moreover, many aspects of these highly specialised institutions are too complex for this book and anyway do not directly concern the general public in the way that banking, insurance and the stock market do.

Other United Kingdom and foreign banks

Besides the London clearing banks, there are other UK banks like the Scottish clearing banks and the Northern Irish banks. Then there are the British overseas and Commonwealth banks, whose deposits are mostly in foreign currency. These banks are based in the City, but their work is largely in Commonwealth and other countries: in particular, they serve British companies working abroad, but they have also developed wider interests and compete with local banks. Some of them are owned – totally or partially – by the four clearing banks.

One of the many overseas banks which have offices in the City

A large collection of foreign banks is now directly represented in London. At the last count, there were some 400 in all, of which seventy-two were from the United States, thirty-five from Japan and 144 were European. They employ almost 40,000 people in London alone. They do not attempt to compete as High Street banks, and only maintain one or two branches in the City itself, but they are very active in the Euro-currency markets and in such business as leasing and factoring.

Finance houses

These institutions, some partly owned by the clearing banks, run the bulk of hire purchase business in this country. By 1983 the total hire purchase debt owed to finance houses had reached £14,000 million.

The usual method of buying goods on 'HP' is that the customer makes a down-payment of a proportion of the price of the goods and then pays the rest in instalments weekly, fortnightly or monthly. Only durable goods like furniture are suitable for this arrangement: the principle of the repayment system is that the value of the debt outstanding at any time should not exceed the second-hand value of the goods at that time. Cars account for most of HP debt.

Building societies

These are non-profit-making organisations specialising in lending money to people to buy their own houses. They borrow from some 28 million depositors and lend to about 6 million borrowers. Hardly any of the societies have their head offices in the City, but they deserve mention here because they dominate the home-loan market in Britain. They are unique to this country and some of them are over 200 years old. Amalgamations have cut their numbers from thousands to about 200, of which the largest five account for over half of all home loans. These large societies have a nationwide branch network, but some of the smaller ones are regional. In all, there are some 6,500 building society branches in the United Kingdom.

In effect, these loans or 'mortgages', as they are called, are just like long-term hire purchase agreements, lasting sometimes as long as thirty years. The societies compete with commercial banks to obtain money for their loans by offering attractive interest rates on deposit accounts, and this rate determines the rate they charge for loans. They allow a margin between the rates to cover administrative expenses and taxation. The societies' assets have grown fivefold in the last ten years and they are eager to extend their activities still further. Some far-reaching changes can be expected before the end of the decade, and legislation to give effect to these changes is already in preparation.

Investment and unit trusts

We have already encountered these trusts in connection with banks and insurance companies, which take a leading part in running them.

Investment trusts, of which there are some 200, are limited companies, some of them dating back to the nineteenth century. The idea behind them is to enable the small saver to own shares in companies without needing specialised knowledge. The trust takes his money in return for its shares and itself buys shares in a very wide range of companies, thus minimising the risk of serious loss if one of the companies should fail. The profits are then paid out as dividends, or else retained in the trust to buy more shares, in which case the trust's shares become more valuable. The total market value of the investments of recognised investment trusts is about £13,400 million.

Unit trusts first appeared in 1931 and there are now about 300 of them. They are authorised by the Department of Trade and Industry and each one is run by a management company, assisted by a trustee company which is usually a bank or an insurance company. They operate by selling 'units' to the general public and the proceeds of the sale are used to purchase company and British Government securities on The Stock Exchange. Ownership of units is not the same as owning shares in the company managing the trust, although it is perfectly possible to do both. The value of unit trust portfolios is now about £13,800 million, compared with £190 million in 1960.

The foreign exchange market

The London foreign exchange market is as big as the next two or three foreign exchange markets put together. Unlike the other exchanges we have looked at, this market occupies no specific premises: dealing takes place over the telephone, between buyers and sellers all over the world. It is by this means that the price of almost every currency is determined. There are two main purposes of dealing in foreign exchange: either to finance trade or to make or save money by speculating on possible changes in currency prices. This speculation performs a useful function in the market by helping to even out the flows of currency.

The Euro-currency market

The size of the Euro-currency market is unknown, but runs into billions of dollars. It has grown up only since the war, but in that short time London has established itself as its undisputed centre. The market works in broadly the same way as the foreign exchange market, except that it is a lending market, not a buying and selling market. Most transactions are in United States dollars, but Deutsche Marks, Swiss francs and sterling are also heavily traded. The term 'Euro' now means merely that the currency is being lent outside its country of origin.

One question which people often ask about the Euro-currency market is this: why would anyone want to borrow foreign money? Why not borrow money in your own currency and, if you need foreign money, buy it in the foreign exchange market? The detailed answer to this question can become very complex, but at its simplest, it is that borrowing Euro-currencies may be cheaper or may involve less risk of loss due to sudden changes in currency values.

The London Commodity Exchange

The London Commodity Exchange is situated just south of Lloyd's in Mark Lane. It is similar to The Stock Exchange in that there are brokers buying and selling on behalf of clients.

The London Commodity Exchange administers a number of futures markets, the principal ones being cocoa, coffee, sugar and oil products. The major purpose of futures markets is to enable the International Trade to hedge or insure their physical commitment to goods. The market is an insurance medium and for that reason less than 1 per cent of contracts, in fact, go through to delivery (although delivery can take place on the futures markets if required). Most deals, therefore, are cancelled out by equal and opposite ones before the delivery date falls due.

The activity of investors or speculators (that is people who are not directly involved in the production or distribution of goods) is an extremely vital, if relatively small, part of the market. If the market was a 'closed' one, there is a grave risk that all the participants would think alike at any one time, in which case there could be no market! Consider, for example, what would happen if everyone in the trade felt that the price was going to fall in the next month. Then everyone would want to sell and no one would want to buy. A market needs people on both sides if it is to work properly and the presence of outsiders who think differently helps to counterbalance the optimism or gloom of those in the business.

The London Commodity Exchange regularly contributes well over £350 million to the United Kingdom's invisible earnings. The turnover is in the region of four times that of The Stock Exchange (excluding Government Securities) and totals about £50 billion per annum.

The Baltic Exchange

The Baltic Exchange is, in fact, the home of several closely related markets. It is situated in St Mary Axe, about as far to the north of Lloyd's as the commodity markets are to the south, and has a floor of some 20,000 square feet. Like the other City markets, it originated in coffee house trading. Here, too, dealing depends on implicit trust in verbal promises. Once a 'fixture' is agreed, that is final. 'Our word, our bond' is the market's unbreakable motto. The Baltic earns Britain some £315 million net a year from abroad.

The 'commodity' traded in chiefly is freight. About 2,700 members, from approximately 700 firms, are engaged in matching the requirements of ship (and aircraft) owners on the one hand and of charterers on the other. It has been estimated that around 60 per cent of the freight shipping of the world is negotiated at some stage by members of the Baltic.

Dealing in 'soft' commodities has always been part of the business of the Exchange. Today there are markets in grain, oil seeds, vegetable and marine oils, and animal fats. Gradually, futures markets have been added, and these include grain, potatoes,

The floor of the Baltic Exchange at the height of the mid-day session

meat (pig and beef), soya bean and in May 1985 the world's first freight futures exchange (BIFFEX – the Baltic International Freight Futures Exchange). There is also a sales and purchases market for ships and aircraft, both new and second-hand.

The London Metal Exchange

Situated in Plantation House, Fenchurch Street, the London Metal Exchange lies right in the heart of the City. The hub of the exchange is a 'ring' some twenty feet in diameter, round which are seated representatives of the City's leading metal merchants. The metals traded are copper, lead, zinc, tin, aluminium, nickel and silver, and their prices are published daily in the financial press.

The London Metal Exchange, or LME for short, is an institution unique to Britain, but it has such world-wide importance that its

Dealers in the 'ring' at the London Metal Exchange

prices for the metals traded on it are recognised as reflecting world prices. As a consequence of the LME's international significance, about half of the seats round the ring are controlled by overseas companies, albeit through British subsidiaries. To become a member and thus control a seat in the ring, a company must produce security of at least £1 million and must be backed by a bank guarantee of a further £500,000, and any further guarantees required by the Board and Committee.

The LME came into being in the second half of the nineteenth century. With the growth of industrialisation on the one hand, and the rapidly rising world output of non-ferrous metals on the other, there had become an urgent need for a proper market in order to stabilise the prices and standardise the quality of these metals. By admitting outside speculators to this market, as with the 'soft' commodities like cocoa, those directly involved in the production and distribution of the metals are assured that they will always be able to buy and sell their goods. The quality of metal traded has to conform to standards laid down by the Committee of the Exchange.

Thus, the LME is a commodity market broadly similar to the ones in Mark Lane. It is a 'spot' or 'cash' market as well as a 'futures' market: that is to say, metals may be bought or sold for delivery next day or for delivery in up to three months. As a generalisation, about 12 to 15 per cent of all deals result in a physical movement of metals. The rest cancel each other out.

Trading on the exchange is done in two main sessions. The morning market lasts from 11.50 a.m. until 1.10 p.m. and the afternoon one from 3.20 p.m. to 4.40 p.m. Unofficial dealings run on for about twenty minutes after each session and are known as 'kerb dealings' from the days when they really did take place on the kerb outside the exchange. The official prices for the metals each day are determined during the morning session and announced after 1.10 p.m.

Industry the world over obviously depends on a regular flow of these essential non-ferrous metals and the LME is a vital link in the chain between producer and consumer. It is all the more astonishing, therefore, to discover that it actually employs only twelve people to manage the day-to-day running of the market.

The bullion market

Prior to the Second World War, London had become the world's leading gold market. The outbreak of hostilities in September 1939 brought the closure of the market and it did not re-open until 1954, so the leadership passed to Zurich and New York. However, by the end of 1955, the London market was handling about four-fifths of the gold that was coming on to the free market anywhere in the world, and that was in spite of the restrictions and difficulties surrounding all international financial markets during the 1950s. The reasons for this rapid re-emergence of London were the small margins and low commissions ($\frac{1}{4}$ per cent for buyers, none for sellers) taken by the City dealers, and the large quantities they were prepared to deal in.

The London market has five members: two are merchant banks, Rothschild and Samuel Montagu; two are brokers, owned by two more merchant banks, and the fifth is a subsidiary of a prominent international metallurgical firm.

Rothschild, though not the largest dealer, is traditionally the senior participant in the market, and as such provides the Chairman and the venue for the daily price-fixing meetings at 10.30 a.m. and 3.00 p.m. Dealings are quoted in dollars and are in 'good delivery bars', which is shorthand for the quality requirements demanded by the London gold market and recognised throughout the world. Rothschild also acts as the Bank of England's agent in the market.

However, a large part of the business of the market is done outside the fixing meetings, with dealers operating over the telephone and the Telex, as in the foreign exchange market. It is quite common for sizeable fluctuations to occur in the price in the course of the day's trading. The advantage of dealing through the fixings is that these meetings provide the nearest thing there is to a perfect market, with many buyers and sellers represented in one room, so that the resulting prices are the most competitive in the world at those times.

Since 1968 the City's leadership in the world gold market has again been challenged, most seriously by Zurich, but also by the growth of the markets in Hong Kong, New York and Chicago. The reason for the much-increased importance of Switzerland has been the decision by South Africa and Russia – the two major gold producers – to dispose of bullion entirely or principally in the Zurich market in recent years.

The financial futures market

The London International Financial Futures Exchange (LIFFE) opened in 1982 in the old Royal Exchange, right in the heart of the City. It works on similar principles to commodity futures markets, except that what is being traded for delivery in the future are standard quantities of financial assets like bonds or currencies. Some 240 banks and other financial institutions are full members of the market.

The method of trading is 'open outcry', that is to say that all transactions must be executed on the floor of the Exchange and prices are instantly available to all participants. A strong voice and plenty of physical stamina are therefore essential qualifications for dealers in this market!

9   Careers and information

A career in the City

The preceding chapters have shown that there is an almost infinite variety of careers in the City for young people today. Even within one profession, e.g. banking, the choices are nearly as wide and it would be an impossible task to compile an exhaustive list. What we can do, however, is select a few types of career and give general details of their structures, opportunities for advancement, entry qualifications and professional examinations, together with the names and addresses of people to write to for further information.

Banking

The High Street banks account for most of Britain's banking business and control over 14,000 branches employing over 300,000 staff. In looking after the 32 million accounts held with them the banks use the latest technology, and are always go ahead in their ideas and in adopting new processes. They have, for example, installed computer systems which are as advanced as any comparable systems in the world. For all that, banking is essentially a matter of dealing with people. They may be industrialists or shopkeepers; more often than not they are private individuals. All are concerned with their own financial affairs; with their money management; with their payment of bills; how to make ends meet. Banks are a source of help and advice for them, organisations through which their cheques are paid, where their savings are looked after and, at times, somewhere to borrow from. In addition to its branches, each bank has many specialist departments which include international, tax, insurance, data processing, personnel, executor and trustee.

Entry qualifications

Not all the banks have the same educational standards of recruitment but generally they like their staff to have a minimum of four academic 'O' levels (or CSE equivalents) including English Language and a numerate subject. Entrants with 'A' levels, the BTEC National Award in Business and Finance and graduates are also recruited. Some banks are now moving towards tiered recruitment and recruits without 'A' levels, or their equivalent, would need to be exceptional in order to reach management.

Training and professional examinations

Experience in banking is gained by undertaking the various jobs within the office, and training is augmented at different stages by instruction given within the office or by courses held at a bank's training centre. In order to be considered for a managerial post it is necessary to pass the Institute of Bankers' examinations.

The educational structure

The examinations are in two stages:
   Stage 1 consists of either a two-year part-time BTEC National Award course in Business and Finance for candidates who have four 'O' levels including English Language, or a one-year part-time conversion course for candidates who have one or more 'A' levels and an 'O' level in English Language. *Stage 2* is a three-year part-time course and to qualify for entry candidates must either

have successfully completed Stage 1 or hold a recognised degree. Full details of the examinations may be obtained from:

The Institute of Bankers,
10 Lombard Street,
London EC3V 9AS.

Remuneration and promotion

Salaries and fringe benefits are attractive. Promotion depends upon ability and performance and applies equally to men and women. Pension and profit-sharing schemes are operated, cheap borrowing facilities are available and an additional allowance is paid to staff working in London and certain other large towns and cities. All the banks have sports clubs and societies catering for leisure activities.
For further information write to:

The Careers Information Adviser,
Banking Information Service,
10 Lombard Street,
London EC3V 9AT.

Insurance

Insurance is also an immensely wide and varied field within which to work. The different skills may be very briefly summarised as follows:
1. Assessing risks so that the premium is a fair charge according to the degree of hazard.
2. Applying actuarial techniques to the calculation of premium rates in life assurance and valuing assets and liabilities.
3. Drawing up insurance policies, which must be legally sound and appropriate to the cover required.
4. Investigating, adjusting and settling losses.
5. Practising marketing and sales administration.
6. Managing investments and property portfolios.
7. Programming and operating computers.

8. Performing servicing functions: accounts, advertising, organisation and methods, personnel, secretarial and training.

As with the other careers listed in this chapter, integrity and the ability to get on with people are first essentials for anyone wanting to enter insurance.

Entry qualifications

Academic requirements are as follows: the usual minimum are either two GCE 'A' level passes or a BTEC National Certificate or Diploma. However, there are also opportunities for school-leavers with GCE 'O' levels in English, Mathematics and at least two other subjects, and such people would normally be expected to study for the BTEC National Certificate by day release. Although most entrants are 'A' level school-leavers, graduates are welcomed in insurance, both for their trained minds, regardless of their particular discipline, and for their specialised ability in Mathematics, Statistics, Law and Economics.

Training and professional examinations

Many insurance employers operate training schemes for new entrants leading to qualification in the Chartered Insurance Institute's Associateship and Fellowship examinations. The Institute has its own College of Insurance, and some companies also run their own training schools. Candidates for the Associateship must pass in nine subjects and Fellowship candidates must pass in a further five subjects chosen from six specialist branches. Most of the larger employers give day release so that their candidates can attend classes at technical colleges.

Remuneration and promotion

Levels of salary, and fringe benefits in insurance cannot be generalised as there are so many employers of such different sizes. But it must be remembered that they have to be competitive with what is offered elsewhere in industry and commerce. Promotion is by merit, and no potential entrant need worry that his efforts will go unrewarded!

For further information write to:

The Careers Information Officer,
The Chartered Insurance Institute,
20 Aldermanbury,
London EC2V 7HY.

Actuary. To become an Actuary in the United Kingdom it is necessary to qualify by examination as a Fellow of either the Institute of Actuaries in London, or the Faculty of Actuaries in Edinburgh. The entry qualifications are harder than for general insurance, and it is now nearly a 'graduate only' profession. For further information write to:

The Assistant Secretary,   or; The Faculty of Actuaries,
The Institute of Actuaries,   23 St Andrews Square,
Staple Inn Hall,   Edinburgh EH2 1AQ.
High Holborn,
London WC1V 7QJ.

Broking. Those specifically interested in insurance broking should write direct to:

The Secretary,
The British Insurance Brokers' Association,
Fountain House,
Fenchurch Street,
London EC3M 5DJ.

Lloyd's of London. For those considering a career in this section of insurance, the appropriate addresses are:

Brokers:
The Executive Secretary,
Lloyd's Insurance Brokers' Committee,
Fountain House,
130 Fenchurch Street,
London EC3M 5DJ.

Underwriters and Corporation staff:
The Personnel Manager,
Corporation of Lloyd's,
London House,
6 London Street,
London EC3R 7AB.

Stockbroking

Stock Exchange firms of either sort, brokers or jobbers, are usually partnerships. They employ staff in three main ways: in dealing, in administration and accounting, and in investment research.

Entry qualifications

There are vacancies in all three areas for candidates from 16 years old upwards, of differing qualifications ranging from 'O' levels to degrees. Except for the few really specialised tasks usually connected with research, academic qualifications are of secondary importance.

Training and advancement

The training of an employee in stockbroking is largely in the hands of his firm. Promotion depends on merit and experience, as well as the size and success of the firm. The newly qualified graduate recruit will often find himself working alongside people of his own age who left school at 16. To become a broker or a jobber one must first become a Member of The Stock Exchange. Only about 4,500 of the 18,000 employed by Stock Exchange firms are members. The aspiring member must have been with his firm for at least three years and be over 21. In addition, if he wants to be a broker he must pass qualifying examinations. With these qualifications, and the support of two existing members to propose and second his application, he is eligible for election by The Stock Exchange Council. On admission, he would be required to pay £1,000 to the

Nomination Redemption Fund and £300 subscription for the current year. These large sums are not, in practice, as big a barrier as they may seem, because it is very common for firms to help out their employees with loans which can be repaid from later earnings.

Remuneration

Salaries vary between firms but in general it can be said that remuneration is always keenly competitive with what is received elsewhere in the City for similar work. In addition many firms pay bonuses when profits are good. For further information, the address to write to is:

> The Secretary,
> The Stock Exchange Clerks' Provident Fund,
> The Stock Exchange,
> London EC2N 1HP.

Visits to City institutions and information services

Anybody who really wants to understand the different City institutions cannot do better than to go and see for himself. The City is only too keen to be understood, and all the institutions mentioned in this book make special arrangements to conduct parties round.

The Bank of England

The Bank offers two types of visit:
1. Educational – for students over the age of 15 studying commerce, economics or business studies. This visit is designed to explain the current role of the Bank and groups may also visit the Bank's museum.
2. General Interest – aimed at individual members of the public and non-educational groups and slanted towards the architecture and history of the Bank.

For further information about the visits above you should

94

telephone the Information Office on 01–601 4444 (Ext. 3832) or write to:

The Information Office,
Bank of England,
Threadneedle Street,
London, EC2R 8AH.

'Career Experience Courses' are also organised by the Staff Office of the Bank – for sixth formers doing at least two academic 'A' level subjects and genuinely interested in the career opportunities for school leavers and Honours graduates (telephone 01–601 4883 or write to the Staff Office at the above address).

The Baltic Exchange

Visitors are allowed by appointment betweeen 11.30 a.m. and 2.30 p.m. Enquiries should be addressed to:

The Secretary,
The Baltic Exchange,
14–20 St Mary Axe,
London EC3A 8BU.

Lloyd's

Enquiries about visits and information should be made by writing to:

The Publicity and Information Department,
Lloyd's,
Lime Street,
London EC3M 7HA.

The Stock Exchange

The visitors' gallery is open between 9.45 a.m. and 3.15 p.m. There are guides and a film lasting about 20 minutes. There is also a stall selling books and dispensing free literature. Entrance: corner of Threadneedle Street and Old Broad Street.

Parties of up to 40 can be accommodated, but the organiser should book his visits in advance by writing to:

The Public Relations Officer,
The Stock Exchange,
London EC2N 1HP.

London Commodity Exchange

For visits and information write to:

The Secretary,
The London Commodity Exchange,
52 Mark Lane,
London EC3R 7NE.

London Metal Exchange

Visits can be arranged between noon and 1.30 p.m. or 3.30 p.m. and 5.10 p.m. Write in the first instance to:

Plantation House,
Fenchurch Street,
London EC3M 3AP.

The financial futures market

The visitors' gallery is open daily from 11 a.m. to 1.45 p.m. For further information telephone 01–623 0444 or write to:

LIFFE Ltd,
Royal Exchange,
London EC3V 3PJ.

Note: None of these places are open over Saturday and Sunday. No charges are made for visits.

Bank Education Service

This is an educational auxiliary sponsored by the London clearing banks to help teachers to provide senior students with factual banking information. For further information, copies of publications or to arrange for a visit by one of its speakers, write to:

The Secretary,
Bank Education Service,
10 Lombard Street,
London EC3V 9AR.

Banking Information Service (Education and Careers)

BIS is an educational liaison organisation sponsored by the High Street banks. Its objective is to help students and teachers become more aware of the role of the banks in the community and to provide information on careers in banking. For further information, resources, or to arrange for a visit by one of its speakers write to:

The Manager,
Banking Information Service,
10 Lombard Street,
London EC3V 9AT.

Bibliography

Introductory

A wide range of explanatory leaflets is published by the various City institutions.

Bank Education Service. Various publications on many aspects of banking business, available free for teachers.

Clarke, William, *Inside the City* (Allen and Unwin, 1979).

Coakley and Harris, *City of Capital* (Blackwell, 1983).

Cockerell, H. A. L. *Insurance* (English Universities Press 'Teach Yourself' Series).

Corporation of London. *City of London* (Ed. J. Burrows & Co. Ltd Publishers, 1972).

Gibson-Jarvie, R. *The City of London: a financial and commercial history* (Woodhead-Faulkner, 1979).

Hodgson, G. *Lloyd's of London* (Allen Lane, 1984).

Irving, Joe. *The City at Work* (André Deutsch, 1981).

McRae, H. and Cairncross, F. *Capital City*, 2nd edition (Eyre Methuen, 1984).

Specialist

Anthony, V. *Banks and Markets* (Heinemann, 1973).

Central Office of Information. *British Banking and Other Financial Institutions* (HMSO).

Clay, C. J. J. and Wheble, B. S. *Modern Merchant Banking* (Woodhead-Faulkner, 1976).

Committee to Review the Functioning of Financial Institutions ('Wilson Committee'). *Report* (HMSO, 1980).

Gillet Bros. *The Bill on London*, revised edition (Methuen, 1977).

Hamilton, J. Dundas. *Stockbroking Today* (Macmillan, 1968).

The London Clearing Banks. *Evidence by the Committee of London Clearing Bankers to the Committee to Review the Functioning of Financial Institutions* (Longman, 1978).

Morgan, E. Victor and others. *Essays on Financial Institutions and Markets in the City of London* (IEA, 1979).

Perry, F. E. *The Elements of Banking*, 2nd edition (Methuen, 1977).

Plender, S. *Financial Institutions and the Nation's Savings* (Deutsch, 1982).

Pringle, R. *Banking in Britain* (Methuen, 1975).

Valentine, S. P. and Mason, S. *Basics of Banking* ('Teach Yourself' Books, 1976).

Glossary

Accepting house: A company which countersigns bills to increase their trustworthiness; 'accepting' renders the 'accepter' liable to redeem the bill if the original signatory (i.e. the drawee) fails to do so when it matures.

Bank: An institution which mediates between borrowers and lenders, accepts deposits and provides a means of transferring deposits by cheque.

Bank of England Intervention Rate: The lowest rate of interest charged by the Bank of England when lending money to members of the discount market.

Bill: A security having a life of one year or less which is sold for less than face value (discount) in order to induce people to purchase it. Gives companies short-term credit at a relatively low cost. The drawee then redeems (repurchases) it at a specified date at face value.

Bond: A certificate received in exchange for a loan, entitling the holder to interest at a fixed rate; usually also names redemption date when holder is entitled to the return of the loan.

Broker: An intermediary between parties to a business transaction.

Clearing bank: A bank which is a member of the London Clearing

House. (There are also Scottish clearing banks, but they do not have a clearing house.)

Clearing House: The place where inter-bank indebtedness arising from the cheque system and bank giro credit system is settled each day. When a cheque has passed through here it is said to have been 'cleared'.

Commercial or trade bill: A bill issued by a company.

Convertible banknote: One that can be exchanged for gold.

Discount house: An institution specialising in making short-term loans by buying bills, using money borrowed from other institutions.

Eligible liability: Sterling deposits with an original maturity of less than two years.

Euro-currency: Any currency owned and lent outside its country of origin.

Euro-dollar: US dollar held and lent outside the United States by persons or institutions not resident in that country. The greater part of Euro-dollars are held here and lent in Europe.

Exchange Equalisation Account: The account at the Bank of England in which are held the United Kingdom's gold and foreign currency reserves. The managers of the account have the task of ensuring that the price of the pound in terms of other currencies is maintained at the level the Treasury wants it to be.

Gilt-edged: Expression used to convey soundness and reliability of a security; officially reserved for UK Government stock.

Instalment credit: A loan which is repayable in regular amounts spread over an agreed period of time: interest is calculated on the whole loan for the whole period and added to the principal before dividing it by the number of repayments to arrive at the amount of each instalment.

Investment trust: A limited joint-stock company using the money subscribed by shareholders to purchase other firms' shares.

Issuing house: An institution which undertakes to launch the shares or other securities of a company.

Jobber: A member of the London Stock Exchange specialising in the purchase and resale of a narrow range of stock and making his living on the 'turn' or difference between his buying prices and his selling prices.

Liquid assets: Assets held by the banks which can be realised quickly to meet sudden demands for cash by depositors.

National debt: The sum of all Central Government debt outstanding.

Reserve assets: Assets of a bank which are specified by the Bank of England in order to comprise the reserve ratio.

Reserve ratio: The ratio of reserve assets to eligible liabilities (broadly deposits) which banks and finance houses must maintain to be approved by the Bank of England.

Special deposits: The deposits made by banks at the Bank of England on its orders, which are frozen until further notice.

Underwriter: One who agrees to accept a risk by signing his name on the form of agreement.

Unit trust: An organisation enabling (mainly small) investors to reduce the risk of loss by investing in a wide range of shares. They are owned and operated by a managing company and they obtain the funds they invest by selling 'units' to the public which can be resold at any time when the market is open.

Yield: The annual cash return on a security expressed as a percentage of what it costs to purchase that security, e.g. a $2\frac{1}{2}$% bond costing £50 yields £5 each year for each £100 invested, which is 5% per annum.